A Fearless Eye:
The Photography of Barbara Ramos

SAN FRANCISCO AND CALIFORNIA, 1969–1973

Essays by
RACHEL KUSHNER,
SALLY STEIN, and
STEVEN A. HELLER

CHRONICLE BOOKS
SAN FRANCISCO

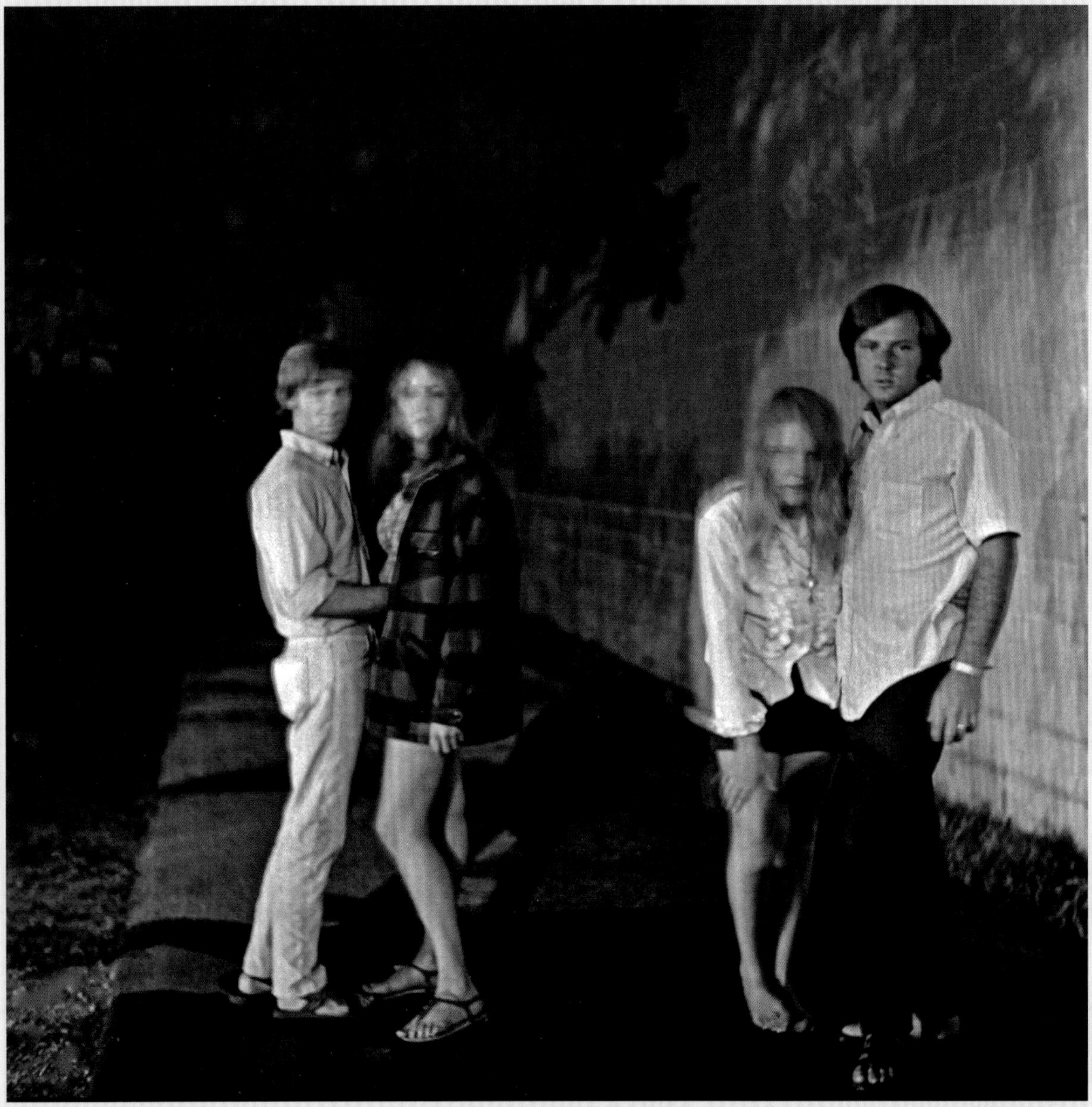

Essays

PREFACE

Rachel Kushner

I arrived in San Francisco at age ten, in the summer of 1979, into the world that these photographs by Barbara Ramos depict. I commenced to wander the city for the next several years, at large and typically alone, enriched with all I needed for a limitless urban independence: bus fare, which at the time, for a school-age minor, was one nickel. Or you could spend your nickel on a late-night transfer, good all day for buses and streetcars, which were sold by men who stood along Market near Civic Center, covertly announcing to passersby, "Late night, late night . . ." They were black market bus transfers, stolen by the book.

I waited an awfully long time for buses in that era. A good portion of my freedom to roam was in fact squandered, spent standing on the cold stone steps of an apartment building entrance waiting for a bus. Standing on a corner, waiting for a bus. Leaning against a wall, waiting for a bus. Just as the people in these photographs, like the young rockabilly family on Sixteenth Street, are waiting still, in some everlasting plane of reality, there is a part of me that is waiting also, and in those very same places. Sometimes I wonder why I didn't walk instead of wait. I have no answer, except maybe the hills, and the way that each neighborhood in San Francisco was comprehensive and discrete, a world unto itself, so that another neighborhood, even if it was a mile away, would be unthinkable except by bus.

On a typical summer day, cold and foggy, and with nothing to do, or on a school day with little to learn, I went downtown and wandered the streets, ducked into head shops to look at their posters for sale, or into the video game parlors if I had money to play. I went to Woolworth's to steal makeup. To the Emporium Capwell for bigger items, a jacket or jeans. I sat on the dry concrete fountain at Civic Center, watching people walk by. Market Street was where shoppers and shoe salesmen, boys with boom boxes, Hare Krishnas and holy rollers hoping for recruits, children and alcoholics, all converged on one broad sidewalk. Most of the people downtown had a place they were going, or, if stationed, a purpose, a mission to sell or to convince. Among this mix, a truant wandering to stare and to notice, and the men with package liquor, were of the same type: outcasts and loiterers. Perhaps it could be argued that the street photographer is also of this special vagrant coterie. The street photographer is moving against the stream, even when she is walking in the same direction as everyone else. She's waiting for her chance, and taking it.

Whether I am looking at the beachgoers in 1930s Nice as photographed by Lisette Model, or the children playing street games in 1940s New York as photographed by Helen Levitt, or the women eating popcorn in San Francisco on the eve of the 1970s as photographed by Barbara Ramos—women who, with their lacquered hair and patent leather, look better equipped for the past instead of the future—in all three milieux, we find photographers seizing upon not what will someday look nostalgic, but what feels alive to them as they get their shot. This is the mystery of good art, that it's almost never about nostalgia, even as part of why we are drawn to great street photography is for the way it gives immortality to scenes that have vanished. It's easy to appreciate and even fetishize the styles of dress and modalities of being of an earlier time, after the fact. It's much harder to see what's interesting about the world you live in. To recognize what's there, in the actually existing present, requires second sight.

The solitary man "sleeping it off" at an unlikely angle on the trunk of an Impala at Altamont, where Sonny Barger and the Hells Angels infamously provided security (and stabbed a man), brings to mind Hunter S. Thompson's depiction of a time when bikers and hippies and Merry Pranksters blended and merged, at least for a spell. By 1969 and 1970, everything is starting to glow a little hotter, to be molded and reshaped by the counterculture, by the Vietnam War, and the sudden withering of postwar conservatism, which offers no allure. The matronly women surrounding a more risqué socialite at the de Young Museum, proud of her own exposed cleavage, seem like they could have been invited to Leonard Bernstein's infamous fundraiser for the Black Panthers.

I remember those little TVs, "personal," mounted at viewing level from rows of molded seats at the Greyhound station, whose entrance was on Sixth Street between Market and Mission. I never saw a woman slunk down in one of those chairs boring into a little TV. It was always men. Those TVs—not yet nostalgic, and instead absolutely modern, even state of the art—seemed so strange to me. Because how could anyone look away from all there was to watch in the Greyhound station, the human drama unfolding every minute? Ramos shows us that the men tunneling into their sports program or their sitcom are part of that drama, even as they try not to be, with the coins they insert, to pay for fifteen or thirty minutes of reprieve from the rest of us.

The stately young Black women rehearsing with their ROTC brigade evoke personal memories for me of high school, and of a time when the city had a more substantial Black population than it does now. Black people have contributed richly to the culture of San Francisco, despite the devastations of urban so-called renewal that took place in the Fillmore, once the epicenter of Bay Area Black life. My high school was twenty percent Black; that same school is now four percent Black. Junior ROTC had a big presence on school grounds and was disproportionately popular with Black students. (Eventually it was discontinued, if recently reinstated.) I was against the military and all it stood for. I despised Ronald Reagan, who was president, and the US imperialism that he symbolized, but I understood that my principles were forged, at least in part, by privilege. (I would be heading to college, unlike most of my classmates.) As the men and women of JROTC, with their straight posture, their creased slacks and braid and berets, rehearsed their synchronized movements on our school's esplanade, my mostly white friends and I, delinquents covertly passing joints and beer cans, watched them, slouched and leaning. The cadets had a pride and forbearance that had nothing to do with the US military, or with any dogma, or even with conformity at all. They moved through their drills without a whiff of war, young people whose elegance and optimism overran the severe aesthetics and narrow dreams of military training.

That's how I remember the women and men of JROTC. And that's what I see still, in the way that Barbara Ramos has captured them here.

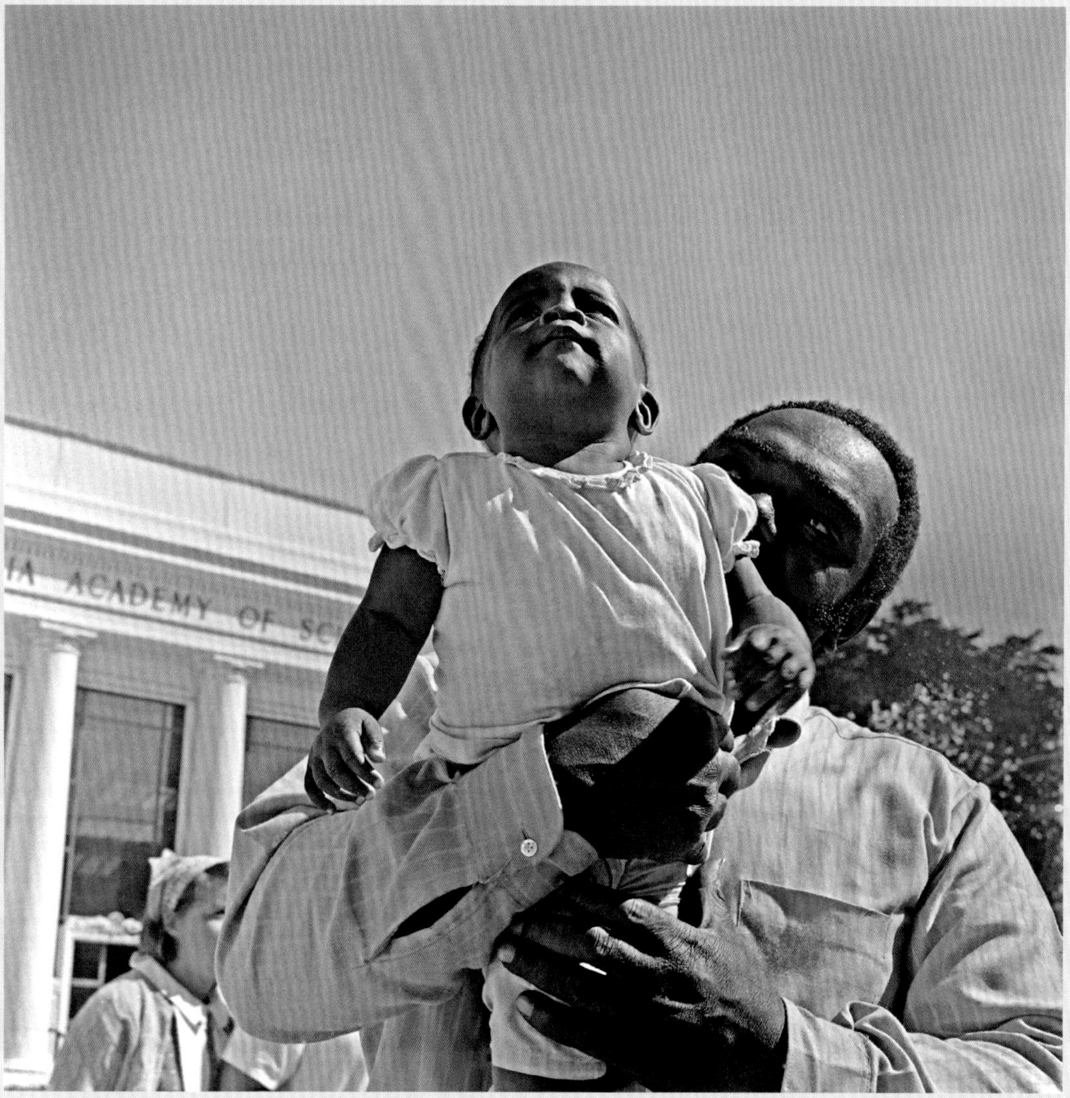
ACADEMY OF

BARBARA RAMOS: A SEPARATE PIECE (AND PEACE) OF STREET PHOTOGRAPHY FROM THE 1970S

Sally Stein

Photographs particularize, often to a degree that sets apart the depicted individual, small group, or unpeopled scene. Yet this was never the isolating effect that Barbara Ramos's photographs had on me, even though starting around 2020 she began presenting on Facebook just one exposure each day from her cache of early-1970s imagery. Quite quickly, her pictures—mainly from San Francisco and the Bay Area but with some made in Los Angeles where she spent her childhood—seemed to link up, like lines of an unfurling poem. I thought I had seen enough photographs to be little moved by new discoveries, yet I was captivated by this unfolding show of largely urban images from a half century earlier.

I still wonder if it was chiefly nostalgia that fueled my interest, and if so nostalgia of what sort? Surely the Spanish surname gave me pause—who is this Latina imagemaker I'd never heard of?—belying the fact that my knowledge of imagemakers is quite limited to a largely Anglo and Western European canon. When I reached out to the source, I quickly learned that Maitles was her maiden, Jewish surname and Ramos is her married name. In the late 1960s while a student at San Francisco Art Institute, she met another art student, Joe Ramos, whose ancestry is both Mexican and Filipino. Joe Ramos is also a notable photographer, although his photography is quite different, being manifestly composed, even when working on the street.

A more decisive factor spurring my interest was the pandemic era of 2020–2023. I first saw her imagery at a time of self-quarantining when I was desperate for anything that promised to restore me to a state of connectedness. Surely isolation in the pandemic contributed strongly to my receptivity, and it also was the basis for Barbara Ramos reconnecting with photography, which she had abandoned nearly fifty years earlier and had long consigned to her "younger self" that had yet to become a self-supporting mature adult.[1] I will return to that break from being a wide-eyed street photographer. First, however, I offer a few thoughts on what struck me strongly on seeing these photographs made relatively long ago, from the time of my own coming of age, which also I learned was the same period of maturation for Barbara Ramos. It turns out we both were born a few years after World War II. Likewise, we both became teens in an era of dramatic change, a time that also inaugurated the term "generation gap."

Originally coined by magazine writer and editor John Poppy for a February 21, 1967, *Look* magazine article, "generation gap" connotes a break, even for some an unbridgeable chasm.[2] Surely people associate this period of the late 1960s with the start of the "Culture Wars." Without a doubt this schism is still with us, arguably even more divisive since Donald Trump's term as the nation's president—a turn of events that surprised so many of us Obama supporters who envisioned a smooth transition from President Barack Obama to President Hillary Clinton. Probably the sharp reaction to our first president who was not a white man should not have taken us supporters by surprise. However, viewed during the pandemic after four years of the next president who relished being as divisive as possible, I began to see in Ramos's photographs from the early 1970s more strains of harmony—of live-and-let-live—than strident discord.

Although I have admired much writing by the late Joan Didion, my appreciation never included her most famous essay, "Slouching Toward Bethlehem" (1967). It was originally written for the *Saturday Evening Post*, and I always felt that fairly conservative platform informs the drift of her text. Her article begins with bits of the W. B. Yeats poem "The Second Coming" (1919)—the selected poetry lines were later replaced with the entire Yeats poem in reprints of collected Didion essays—that gave rise to her "Slouching" title, while omitting such key phrases as "The best lack all conviction, while the worst / Are full of passionate intensity." The hippies on whom Didion focuses seem more dazed and drug-addled than full of passionate intensity. Moreover, Didion pays little attention to the major causes for "dropping out" in the late 1960s: the multiple assassinations of leaders who advocated for change, the drafting of young men into a senseless war, the recent challenges to both white and male supremacy. In a 1965 essay from this period, Didion confesses her fondness for a rearguard hero like John Wayne.[3] But arguably the most tendentious aspect of this reportage is how it concludes by dwelling on an incident of a mother who feeds her young child psychedelics and dubs this experiment "High Kindergarten." In that finale, a child had suffered burns, thankfully not too severe, when he apparently under the influence of drugs bit into electrical wires. No matter that this precedes a period of near ubiquitous childproofing, the mother in question has clearly abdicated responsibility. Yet the author's focus on this exceptional scene of dysfunctional parenting seems designed to smear all nonconformists of this "New Age" as unfit for most adult roles. Especially so as her closer in this reportage is an arresting vision of a generation incapable of nurturing a future, up there with the Goya's most vivid image of *Saturn devouring his son* (1818–1823).[4]

Ramos, by contrast, offers no scenes so electrifying nor any view that leers sardonically, which was a staple of the predominantly male genre of street photography.[5] Those peopling her multifaceted chronicle seem intent on finding their way in a city renowned for its diversity, economic as well as ethnic. Some depicted look like they may reside in capacious Victorian homes, for which San Francisco is justly famous, or else in the suburbs, but many also seem likely to be denizens of rooming houses. Some progress achieved by new civil rights legislation is reflected in a fancy department store scene in which a young Black boy is welcomed by a Black man working the counter (page 36). Backlash to that same gradual progress of civil rights is suggested in one scene in which a conventional ROTC military drill involving Black students is suddenly disrupted by an unexpected threat from outside the frame (page 68). The cast of urban characters includes quite a few out-of-town tourists, yet they seem far less judgmental than Didion, rather simply curious. The young appear hopeful while elders tend to look more regretful, but not always; there's one electric exchange of glances between an old woman and man who still seem to possess joie de vivre, thus eroding generation gap stereotypes (page 37).

People displaying or waving flags are rare. This is far from Robert Frank's view of 1950s Cold War America in which the flag figures as binding and blinding motif. Likewise, when we are presented with a few scenes of boys with toy guns, there's no sense of intense menace that William Klein sought with his portrait of a boy with gun mirroring his own aggressive shooting with camera.[6] In Ramos's encounter, the boys look like they are enjoying the gentle face-off with as many grins as juvenile bravado (page 29).

While the flag has diminished importance, the romance with cars abounds—one view by Ramos features a billboard that actually promises the car may become your most dependable friend (page 70).

Nevertheless, she makes nearly as many pictures of riders of public transport who appear reasonably contented with this more communal form of transit. Keep in mind that these pictures were made before the OAPEC embargo in the second half of 1973 quadrupled the cost of gasoline at the pump, blowing a hole in the fantasy of automotive liberation, not to mention putting an end to the Big Three motor companies' unconditional success with oversize gas guzzlers (which of course led to a major downturn for the US workforce in the automotive industry). In retrospect these first years of the 1970s are a fairly tranquil interlude between all the hoopla around the 1967 Summer of Love and before Harvey Milk, the first openly gay San Francisco city supervisor, was assassinated in 1978, one year after his taking office. This period also precedes the tragic deaths of the HIV-AIDs crisis that cast a pall over San Francisco, which had been a mecca for gays. Equally hard to foresee in these pictures is the gentrification combined with the Silicon Valley boom that drove nearly all but the upper class out of the city. However exceptional, I could not help but be charmed by her capture of a time that did not seem rocked by crisis. Instead, it offered a glimpse of a society brewing with diversity yet, notwithstanding Yeats's image of impending dissolution, the center still held. The brew had not congealed into factions at each other's throats, which certainly seems to be the divisible state of affairs in 2024.

As late as the early 1990s, James Davison Hunter could still write a thick but eminently readable analysis about America's Culture Wars that concludes with hopes for the efficacy of tolerant pluralism mending the societal rifts that threatened our democracy.[7] For many reasons, starting with the hollowing out of decent working-class jobs as corporations sought cheaper production overseas, combined with the rise of new media channels that constantly worked the demonizing effect of scapegoats, Hunter's most reasonable hopes for "moral pluralism" seem like pipe dreams. But especially in the early 1970s as framed by Ramos, allowance for diversity seems the order of the day, and a saving grace.

Her photographs do not avoid sensational conflict. Instead they allude to conflictual possibilities in a restrained manner. Numerous photographs do contain their own potential for explosive friction. A photograph pitting lions and lambs could easily have been made of her scene of the aftermath of the infamous concert at Altamont Speedway where the Rolling Stones quite recklessly hired Hells Angels to keep the peace. Instead, one of these ad hoc guardians of security fatally stabbed one Black man and injured dozens of others. To compound the horror, the main perpetrator was later acquitted of malfeasance.[8] I asked the photographer who attended that concert if she had seen the attack; and if not, did she even know about it since her photograph avoids condemnation?

No, I learned, she was too far from the stage to see the attack but the word had spread fast so she certainly had heard something about it when late in the day she encountered a young man seeking to catch up on sleep after a long stay at the concert (page 31). The photographer might have let the boy slip out of focus so she could capture the bikers and their machines in the background (who likely were not Hells Angels). But instead she focused close on the sweet-faced youth, letting the signs of bikers and choppers remain a distant, only half-threatening figuration.

Similarly, peace, not mayhem, informs the spirit of the crowd on the street waiting to enter a screening of *The Exorcist*, which scene she later titled *Waiting for the Exorcist* (page 90). Hardly anyone foresaw that William Friedkin's 1973 horror film would quickly become a blockbuster success, inspiring a new cult genre. It is as if instead of possession stigmatizing a single person, there is consensus that we were all or at least many of us slightly possessed by bad dreams, bad karma, following the 1960s that had left us shocked by multiple assassinations and thousands of young men killed or traumatized after being dispatched to fight a war they were promised would result in a victory for democracy. Already in the 1950s, San Francisco was the seedbed for a poem with multiple refrains of the singular "I," waiting out the anomie for a "rebirth of wonder."[9] Here a crowd waits patiently for collective catharsis.

The orderly lineup for *The Exorcist* notwithstanding, numerous pictures by Ramos seem to insist that true revelation can't be staged or scripted in advance. I'm referring first of all to two pictures I quickly twinned in my head as a most effective diptych (pages 78–79). One shot inside an art school classroom shows an older man working hard to capture the entwined poses of two naked female models, and despite the low light of this interior, the photographer manages to capture both foreground and background as equally readable and significant. That's the predictable studio, and it seems rather suffocatingly dull—a commentary by a fairly alienated art student whose second shot serves as mocking retort to this academic environment. In that riposte, two women are caught in the act of play-wrestling with their arms (I imagine one is commenting on the hair color or cut of the other, and the second is jokingly swatting back at this interlocutor). They are fully dressed and seem so much more alive and truly interactive than the posed duo of naked models. Ramos captures their jocular interplay while partly obscuring the male figure behind them. In situ, she seems to say, there's greater possibility for seeing a true rapprochement in everyday life than on the stage or screen or in a book.

Another photograph delivers a similar message that the unplanned action potentially yields the greatest surprise. Ramos happened upon an unannounced museum event where art donor Tullah Hanley takes over the sedate environment with a surprise show at the 1970 opening of an exhibition at the de Young Museum of paintings that Hanley donated to the museum following her older husband's death. The elder ladies in their good cloth coats surrounding the scantily garbed, merry widow appear quite amused. They are not about to shed their clothing, but no one looks too scandalized by this ad hoc bit of performance art by a former belly dancer who charmed a millionaire into marrying her. If anyone looks judgmental, it is the peering eye of George Washington in the nearly obscured Rembrandt Peale painted portrait (page 42). Needless to say, the watchful stare of the Founding Father hardly subdues this gathering.[10]

Ramos finds pleasure when shock is present while kept restrained in her pictures. In the image at a Peace Rally (page 81), this photographer has framed the scene to divide nearly equally between left and right sides. On the left, two men embrace with gusto; on the right, one old woman hugs herself while rather grimly looking away, and the man behind her looks at the young male couple with maybe more curiosity yet possibly also simple resignation at this frank, public display of affection. However, looking away seems the strongest reaction. Officially it's a scene of protest on behalf of peace, and nobody in her scene is protesting this behavioral schism. Tolerance prevails despite the compositional divide.

Likely owing to this lack of raw shock, these photographs did not find an immediate audience with those who favored sensationalism. Ramos felt ignored at the San Francisco Art Institute (SFAI) or else treated as Joe's sidekick. A small show of prints she installed in a hallway gallery of the art school generated no response from either teachers or fellow students. When one of the instructors—Richard Conrat, a former assistant to Dorothea Lange, planning his own book on California agriculture—pressed Joe Ramos to focus on his farmworker roots in the Salinas area in the hopes he might contribute to the envisioned book, Conrat joked that if Joe resisted this suggestion, he might try to dispatch Ramos to make pictures in Salinas. Since the Valley she grew up in was the suburban sprawl of Los Angeles, she, in this context, felt like little more than a joke decoy. When Joe and Barbara brought their prints to Annie Leibovitz, who, while still completing her BFA at SFAI, had begun working at *Rolling Stone* magazine as both a photographer and picture editor, Leibovitz chose one of Joe's pictures but completely passed on the work Barbara brought for consideration. No wonder that Ramos, who always preferred the street to the darkroom, ceased making most prints when they only added to her sense of being overlooked. She took away the idea that, especially with street photography, her prospects were slim at best. Maybe it seemed that the sole spot for a woman pursuing this path had been occupied by Diane Arbus (1923–1971), who, before her death, had been one of three photographers hailed at MoMA in a show called *New Documents* (1967). The way the world worked at the time—and frequently still does today—one woman may have seemed more than enough in a category like street photography that was historically occupied by men.

Sometime by the mid-1970s, after stints as a nightclub photographer at the staid Fairmont Hotel and the racier Finocchio's, and a separate stint managing "The Fun Terminal," which also involved changing the short reels of skin flicks, Ramos resolved to put aside her camera for good. Her father was a lifelong leftist who brought his family west to Los Angeles for work as a publicist in the movie industry, for a while even heading the CIO guild of movie publicists. He believed that work should be meaningful, self-respecting, and decently paid. Around the time Barbara married Joe in 1975, they resolved to collaborate on various craft enterprises. Together they had surprising success making and selling masks that often riffed on Chicano types like "The Vato," also combining masks with pinwheels that they marketed as "Windalas" (which likely riffed on the exotic hippie fad for eastern mandalas). For a few years they did remarkably well with those items and then they switched to handmade jewelry. Ramos grew enchanted, obsessed even, with fine glass beads, searching out wholesalers specializing in antique stockpiles of tiny beads in subtle but shimmering colors. She and Joe did the beadwork, Joe managed publicity, and together they sold the intricate jewelry at craft fairs throughout the West and Southwest. With much time on the road, setting up their booth, interacting with customers (many of whom became devoted regulars), they supported themselves and their two children, no less in an old San Francisco house (albeit in the Richmond neighborhood notable for its persistent foggy weather) that they secured with a down payment from their sales. Four decades later, that venerable house remains their home, which they keep filled with treasures self-made, found, and traded, with still a stockpile of beads she has stopped working with but has yet to give away. They only ended the jewelry business after forty years of taking their wares on the road on a regular schedule of regional craft shows. When shortly later the pandemic hit, Joe suggested to Barbara that she use the enforced isolation at home to turn the internet into a photo platform. The photographs she had made a half century prior quickly turned heads, including Steven A. Heller's and mine. There's more than a little irony that in a period when photographers would do most anything for a publication, her work finds its way from negatives to book form without multiple intermediary trials of countless exhibitions and maquettes. The art world like the rest of the world is unpredictable. Sometimes attention arises just because the work once released to the world on something so insubstantial as the virtual internet calls for a more permanent inscription. More than the simple rediscovery of pictures from a half century ago is the vision of a world that contained notable crevices but had not exploded beyond the possibility of cohesion. Given this unexpected response, she has begun photographing again, seeking to capture anew a deeply familiar but greatly changed locale.

I find it aptly coincidental that as I draft this essay, a message pops up on my screen quoting the current governor of the border state of Texas: "The only thing we're not doing is shooting people."[11] That official declaration follows state guards claiming to see no sign of a mother and her children drowning in the Rio Grande while the troops were massed on the border to block all attempted entries. At least this governor refers to the migrants as people, but the policies of refusing to offer any aid to those making a perilous journey is a tacit form of dehumanization.

A little more than a decade ago, esteemed photography curator Anne Wilkes Tucker organized a widely touted exhibition titled *War/Photography.* Preoccupied with my partner's terminal illness, I missed the exhibit but followed its reception online and ordered the catalog that was heavy in all senses.[12] After studying that volume intently, I wrote appreciatively to the curator while also noting that now I hoped to see a companion work on *Peace/Photography.* That admittedly seemed a harder topic. I myself had trouble envisioning many pictures that might be so grouped other than W. Eugene Smith's "A Walk to Paradise Garden," which served as visual epilogue to Edward Steichen's *Family of Man* exhibition and book of 1955, or Marc Riboud's 1967 scene of an earnest peace protester offering flowers to a soldier wielding a rifle with fixed bayonet. With a nod to Ferlinghetti, I am still waiting for an exhibition of *Peace/Photography*. Yet after spending time with Ramos's depiction of the Bay Area a few years after the putative "Summer of Love"—her pictures leading me to reread both Joan Didion on the Hippie Generation and James Davison Hunter's more judicious analysis of our Culture Wars—I know a bit better that what I seek is more images suggesting (not dictating) how we might live tolerably with our differences.

Notes

[1] Ramos discusses at greater length her early renunciation of photography in the essay combined with an interview by Steven A. Heller, included in this volume.

[2] On the origins of the term by Poppy, who claimed he was drawing on the widely cited "missile gap" assessing US–Soviet military might, see Lisa Marsh Ryerson's July 13, 2016, piece in the *Huffington Post*, "Do You Remember the Generation Gap?"

[3] Joan Didion, "John Wayne: A Love Song," reprinted in the *Slouching Toward Bethlehem* volume of early Didion essays published by Farrar, Strauss in 1968.

[4] This most famous of the "Black Painting" late series by Francisco de Goya y Lucientes is housed at the Prado in Madrid and can be viewed via its online collection.

[5] Colin Westerbeck and Joel Meyerowitz's *Bystander: A History of Street Photography* (Little, Brown, 1994) offers an invaluable survey of this photographic genre. The best critique of this genre remains Patricia Vettel Becker's *Shooting from the Hip: Photography, Masculinity and Postwar America* (University of Minnesota Press, 2005), in addition to the feminist essays on the gendered photography of Garry Winogrand and the title he favored for his second published series capturing females on the street: *Confessions* of a Male Chauvinist Pig: Rethinking Winogrand's Women* (California Museum of Photography, 2013).

[6] This 1954 photograph by Klein appears on the cover of some editions of his New York book, first published in 1956, and is easily found online as part of the collection of the Metropolitan Museum.

[7] James Davison Hunter, *Culture Wars / The Struggle to Define America / Making Sense of the Battles over the Family, Art, Education, Law, and Politics* (New York, Harper Collins, 1991); see especially the final "Toward a Resolution" section, 295–325.

[8] Sasha Frere-Jones, "The Chaos of Altamont and the Murder of Meredith Hunter," *New Yorker*, March 28, 2019.

[9] On San Francisco poet, publisher, and indie bookstore cofounder Lawrence Ferlinghetti and his most famous poem of 1958, "I Am Waiting," see both the poem in its entirety and a biographical essay on the Poetry Foundation website.

[10] For an aptly colorful, contemporary verbal portrait of a determinedly shocking Tullah Hanley, see a January 23, 1970, piece by San Francisco journalist Herb Caen reprinted online by *SFGate*.

[11] Press release, Children's Defense Fund, January 12, 2024, "CDF-Texas Condemns Violent Language from Governor Abbott Regarding People Crossing the U.S.-Mexico Border."

[12] Anne Wilkes Tucker, Wills Michel, Natalie Zelt, *War/Photography: Images of Armed Conflict and Its Aftermath* (Houston Museum of Fine Arts, 2012).

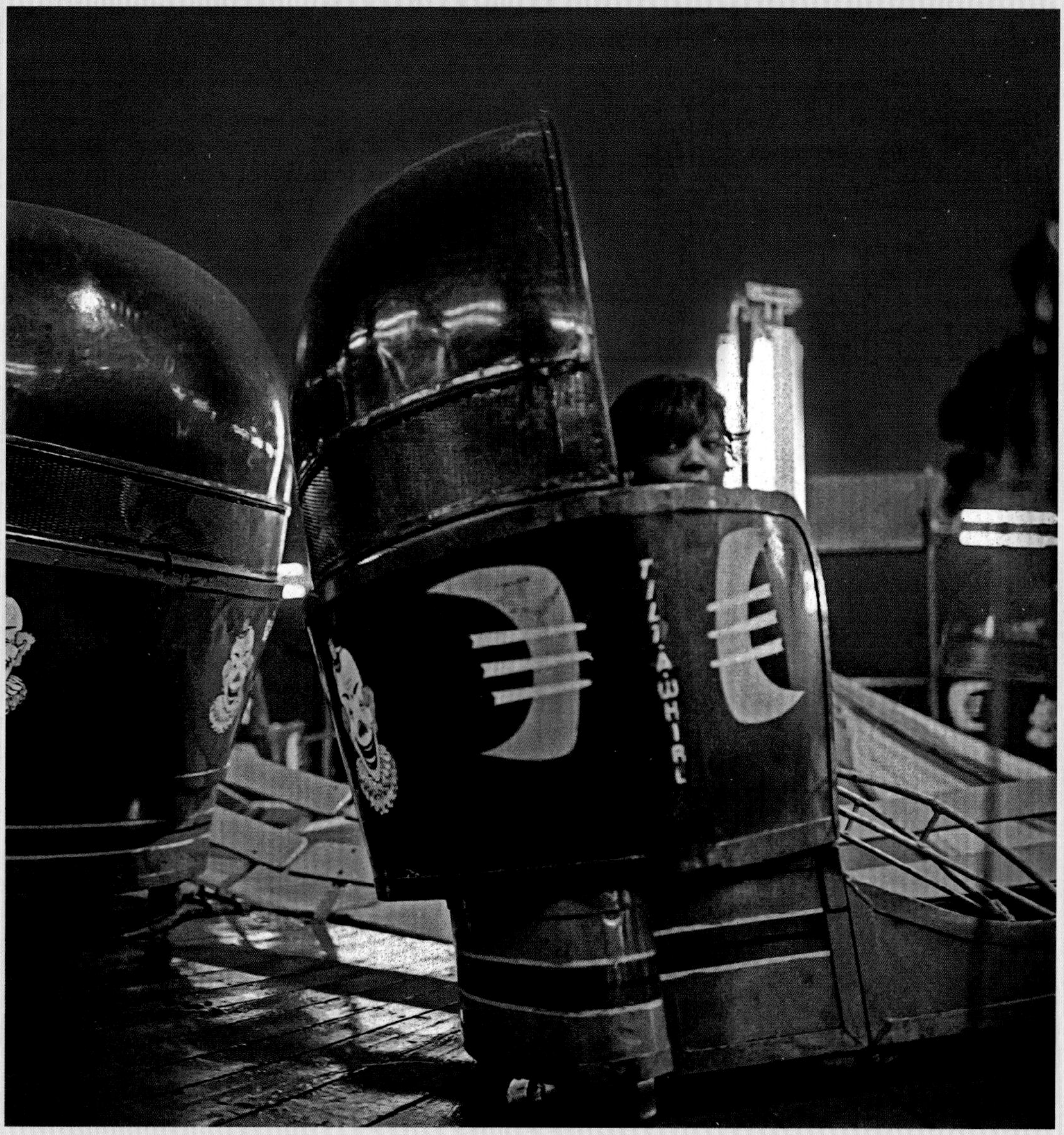
TILT-A-WHIRL

BARBARA RAMOS: A FEARLESS EYE

Steven A. Heller

This is a story best told by the photographer herself, Barbara Ramos, as it is entirely unique and destined to become an integral factual account of a journey that few in the 195-plus years of photography's history have been able to recount from the first-person perspective. After nearly fifty years of silence, the work of Barbara Ramos looms on the horizon of enormous and well-deserved recognition.

At the edges of time there can be discovered caches of information and goods deliberately or in some cases unintentionally hidden as a means of communicating with the future. The concept (or ritual) dates back three thousand years and occupies a central role as the prototype of written literature. Inscribed in ancient cuneiform on twelve clay tablets—discovered in 1849—the poetic classic *Epic of Gilgamesh* tells of gods and mortal Mesopotamians, locked in love, religion, and political struggle. Forgotten and dislocated during the turmoil of frequent military battles and time, it is now considered a significant influence on Homer's narratives of *The Iliad* and *The Odyssey*. Collectively, archeologists, religious scholars, and anthropologists regard *Gilgamesh* as the earliest historical reference of a "time capsule" lost and found.

Suppose that every photograph ever taken since Niépce's view from the window at Le Gras in 1826 would be considered a time capsule unto itself waiting to be lost and ultimately rediscovered? Suppose every nuance, grain, and pixel of knowledge in that photograph revealed something previously unknown or forgotten until prompted by the visual reference? Suppose that is the underlying philosophy of the photographic medium waiting at the edges of time to be told?

Over the course of several months, I had the exclusive opportunity for in-depth interviews with Barbara Ramos as she looked back almost half a century to revisit imagery that had been hidden away, much as the clay tablets of the Gilgamesh epic. Born in New York City, Ramos was the youngest member of her family, who moved to Los Angeles when she was six. Her father worked in the film industry, conceiving, writing, producing, and editing trailers for coming attractions. "I never thought of him as being visual, but in reality, he was," she says. "It was exciting to walk through the sets with him, and it made a great impact on me. At home, I saw black-and-white photographic stills on his worktable, but I wasn't able to connect to them at the time."

Reflecting on Ramos's imagery, it is impossible not to imagine that some place in her subconscious all of this work left an indelible visual foundation. Ramos was "perplexed" by the technical aspects of the medium when taking her first photographs in the late 1960s. Another challenge was one she shared with many women back then in that "photography was a male-dominated competitive culture"—a culture she did not feel equipped to deal with. Yet, despite these hurdles, from the moment she picked up a camera, the medium commanded her total attention and commitment.

A baby-boomer child who often felt shy around people, Ramos discovered after moving to San Francisco a world she had never known growing up in Los Angeles, and decided to attend the San Francisco Art Institute in 1969. Although missing the quirky people and light of Southern California, she found that her shyness quickly disappeared, and "I had no problem going up to strangers and taking their photograph."

The trade-off was that, despite its "flower child" reputation in the popular imagination, the bulk of San Francisco in fact seemed too conservative, the architecture lacked character, and "the light was too gray." Following art school and then a graduate degree at San Francisco State, Ramos confronted one of the more difficult aspects of life—how to make a living and at the same time raise a family.

Like many photographers, growing up Ramos considered herself an "observer" within her family environment. She had a passion for drawing, painting, and, at an early age, "drawing sequences of pictures of people doing everyday things like brushing teeth or combing hair."

These sequences served as the subject matter for little books that Ramos created. Looking back on this creative activity, she believes that her photographs are actually vignettes for longer, more-detailed stories wherein gestures and facial expressions transform a captured moment into a narrative. Comparing those childhood drawings with the adult's street photos, it is evident that Ramos has sealed an envelope of movement and activity that her subjects have surrendered to the lens.

Ramos recalls, "From the beginning, I found the act of photographing a very athletic activity. I don't stand still when I photograph. I am participating in the photo. During my college years in Los Angeles, I worked in a couple of photo labs, and in San Francisco I worked as a 'camera girl' photographing tourists at the Fairmont Hotel, Top of the Mark, and Finocchio's [nightclub]. The reality of being a photographer and being told what to photograph was not something I wanted to do. In a way, I felt I became like the people I was photographing; I became the photograph. Every waking minute I was obsessed by looking, by exploring the world. It was always exciting to look at the negatives, which I developed myself, although I rarely proofed or printed. But my negatives from this body of work were literally hidden away in cardboard boxes for five decades. I became intensely involved in making a living in an art jewelry business—still visually creative, but in a more decorative and commercial form. It was the pandemic that forced me to confront my past."

At the urging and support of her husband, Ramos began the painstaking task of editing through boxes of negatives and taking advantage of the pandemic restrictions to begin digitizing the work. The process evolved into a newfound level of encouragement and admiration as she began to post the work on social media platforms. "Forty-five years ago, I began to throw away some negatives, but my husband immediately retrieved them from the garbage. After that, I just put them away in boxes; out of sight, out of mind. It was my husband, Covid, and plenty of time on my hands that signaled the return to that former photographer I had been so consumed with becoming."

When probed to confront the possibility that the work might never see the light of day beyond the storage boxes, Ramos is clear about the outcome. "First, I never would have thrown away my negatives. I guess the negatives represented my subconscious, and I didn't want to deal with that part of myself, let alone letting other people see that, including my family. I think that is the human condition. I don't think it's that unusual. It is probably why people can identify with the stories in the photos. We all have parts of ourselves hidden away, even if we don't realize it. I think that is what my photography is all about. As to the pandemic, you have to remember I have worked nonstop my entire adult life. Anything that would have given me space would have led me back to my negatives."

Ramos's journey bears a striking resemblance to that of Vivian Maier's lifelong secret obsession with photography—there are numerous parallels between the women, from their obsession with street photography to the "rediscovery" of their private archives—while her vision, perhaps, shares more in common with such legends as Robert Frank, Diane Arbus, Mary Ellen Mark, Lee Friedlander, and Henri Cartier-Bresson. Looking over her shoulder at the work of these influential photographers, Ramos strives to [re]discover her influences and distinctions. "I saw Cartier-Bresson's photography as purely art, and understood the intentions," she muses. "I identified with Frank as the 'outsider looking in,' but I also saw the quirky, even surreal scenes that puzzled me. Arbus and Mark, often working on assignments, knew how to direct a photo; I often felt part of the photograph and didn't direct people, simply because they were often moving elements of the situation. I basically worked with abandon, without restrictions. I can see how [Maier's] work is similar to mine, as we both had an intense curiosity about mostly urban people in urban environments."

The photographic archive Ramos produced is nothing short of remarkable, especially when viewed in the context of legendary exponents of documentary, bystanders, and street photography genres. "During my fifty-year hiatus from photography I didn't look at any photo books or exhibitions. It's almost impossible to put into words the reasons. Maybe I thought photography was just part of my former younger self."

It is the fairly recent discovery of Vivian Maier's work that seems to have the most direct correlation to Ramos. "Maier was obsessive with the camera, and like me had no assignments. She kept her work to herself, and apparently had little concern with technique. Our hermit sensibilities, and the need for privacy which steered our passion, highlight the similarities of our work."

The issue of "privacy" for most photographers is quite paradoxical, especially given today's instantaneous ability to upload images to social media and update websites. How did it come to happen that Ramos's archive has been invisible all these years?

"As far as me abruptly stopping photographing, I can honestly say I don't know why," Ramos states. "It wasn't as though I wasn't still seeing; I just didn't photograph. It was painful for me to not photograph, and truth be told, I was very private about my work. I just wasn't ready to bring attention to myself."

Ramos and her husband established a successful jewelry design business in the early 1970s. In tandem with raising two children, life proved challenging. Ramos's husband, Joe, is also a photographer, of Filipino and Mexican descent; Ramos's background is a white Jewish family. "It's difficult to understand, but when Joe and I would travel doing our jewelry business, I was the one who had to register at the motel desk if we were to get a room for the night. Our children being triracial had to deal with fitting into a white Anglo world. This all added to the conflict of prioritizing where my energies would best be applied. I literally did not pick up a camera. I had somewhat of a phobia about not having the ability to photograph once I'd stopped."
Ramos's gifted vision is apparent in full force as her negative archive is further unearthed. The images, startling in their humanity, objectivity, and originality, deserve to share center stage with those of Frank, Maier, Arbus, and Friedlander.
Her photographs connect without hesitation. Many of her images of people on the street might easily be frames from Frank's *The Americans* for their sense of looking deeper into the passing parade of faces and forms. "Often when I photographed, I would get into a zone, especially in busy downtown areas of San Francisco," Ramos recalls.
Ramos may have had misgivings about San Francisco as a prime opportunity for street photography, yet in the city's neighborhoods—North Beach, Chinatown, downtown near Market Street, even on the bus—she made amazing captures teeming with atmosphere and authenticity. "I spent a lot of time between North Beach and Chinatown, because both were very close to the San Francisco

Art Institute where I was studying photography."

Many of the images derive their impact from their subjects' direct engagement with Ramos. She frequently catches them with freeze-frame candor gazing directly at her camera, their expressions by turns startled, wary, bemused, annoyed, or various combinations thereof. Willingly or unwillingly, they engage in a kind of unspoken communication with the audacious woman taking their photograph; these metaphysical exchanges provide fascinating entry points for the viewer.

As our exchange continued, Ramos seemed as much reflective of her past as she was stimulated by the present. And that seems appropriate to the eight stages of human development that psychologist Erik Erikson theorized in the 1960s. According to Erikson, it is in this eighth "chapter" that individuals must learn to accept the course of their life or they will look back at it in despair. "Ego integrity" is what he identified as the acceptance of life in its fullness; the victories, defeats, and associated wisdom.

Barbara Ramos finds herself wondering what happened to many of the people she photographed. "Interestingly, when I posted a photograph on Facebook of a window dresser in downtown San Francisco Macy's department store, a friend recognized the man in the window. He told me that he was a friend of his and that he'd recently passed away. My friend gave me the address of his sister and I sent her a print of the image."

Today Ramos is more consumed with photography than perhaps at any previous point in her life. Working with a digital camera and back on the streets of the city, she is acutely aware of the changes that have taken place over these fifty years of technology.

"There is a difference between my street photography of the past and my current approach. Back then I was fully interacting with my subjects. Now I'm very conscious of the changing environment they have to navigate. In the past people were comfortable in their environment; now it seems that many people are wandering unsure of where to be. It was a give-and-take experience fifty years ago and I still experience some of that. But today people are more cautious about being photographed."

Plates

All photographs were taken between 1969 and 1973.
All were taken in San Francisco unless otherwise noted.

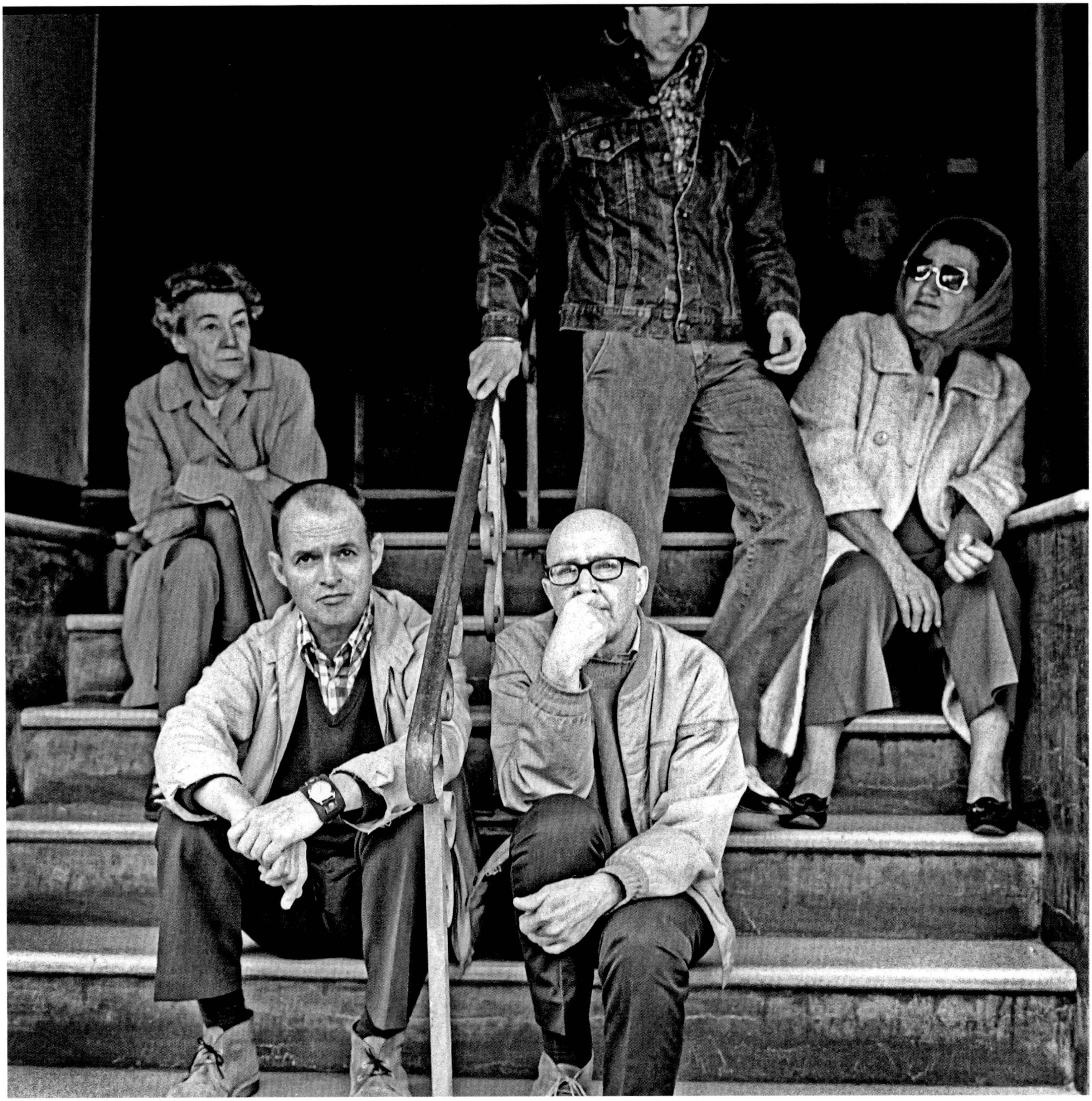

Waiting for the Bus, Nob Hill

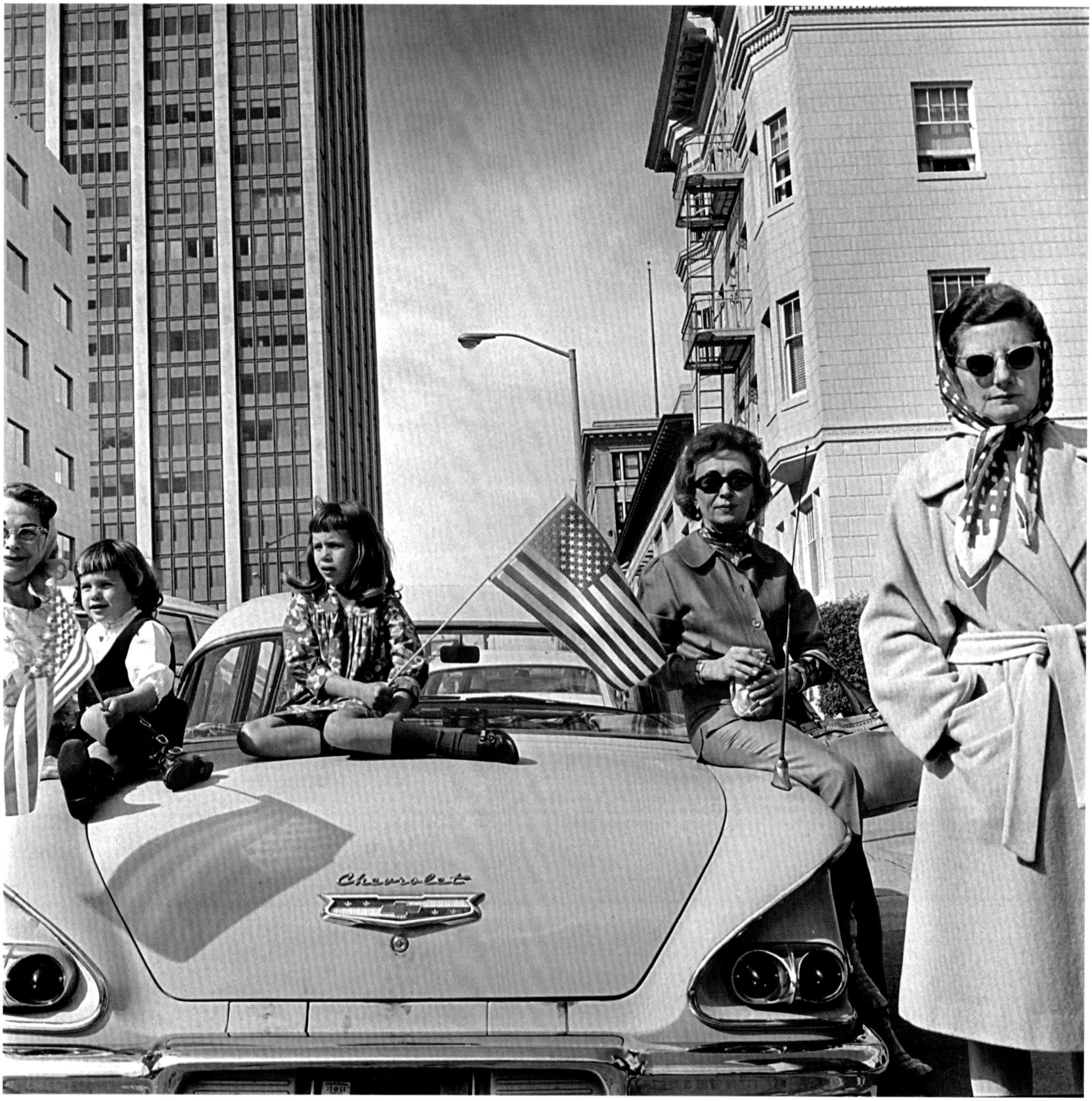

Veteran's Day, Civic Center

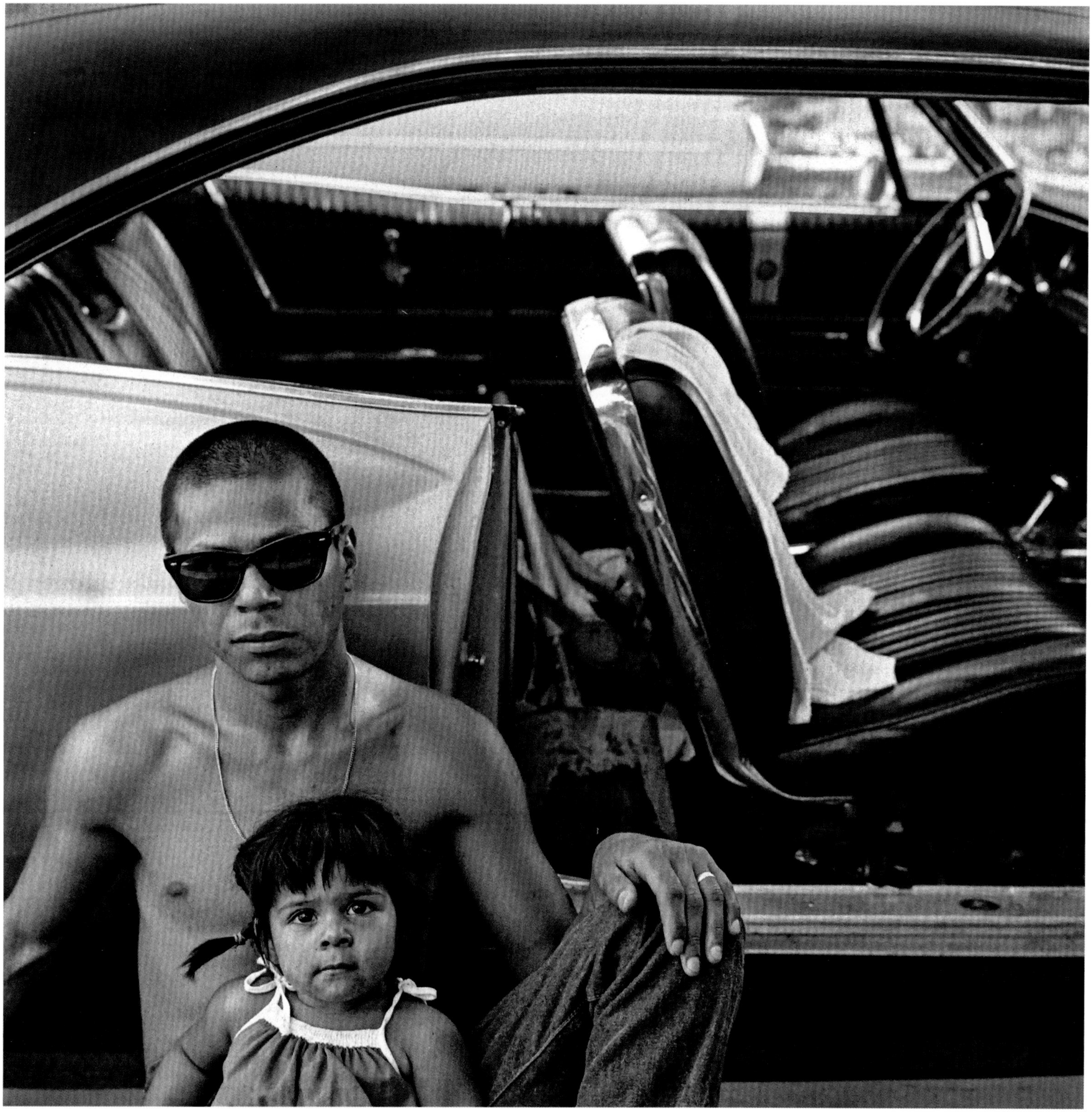

Father and Daughter and Car

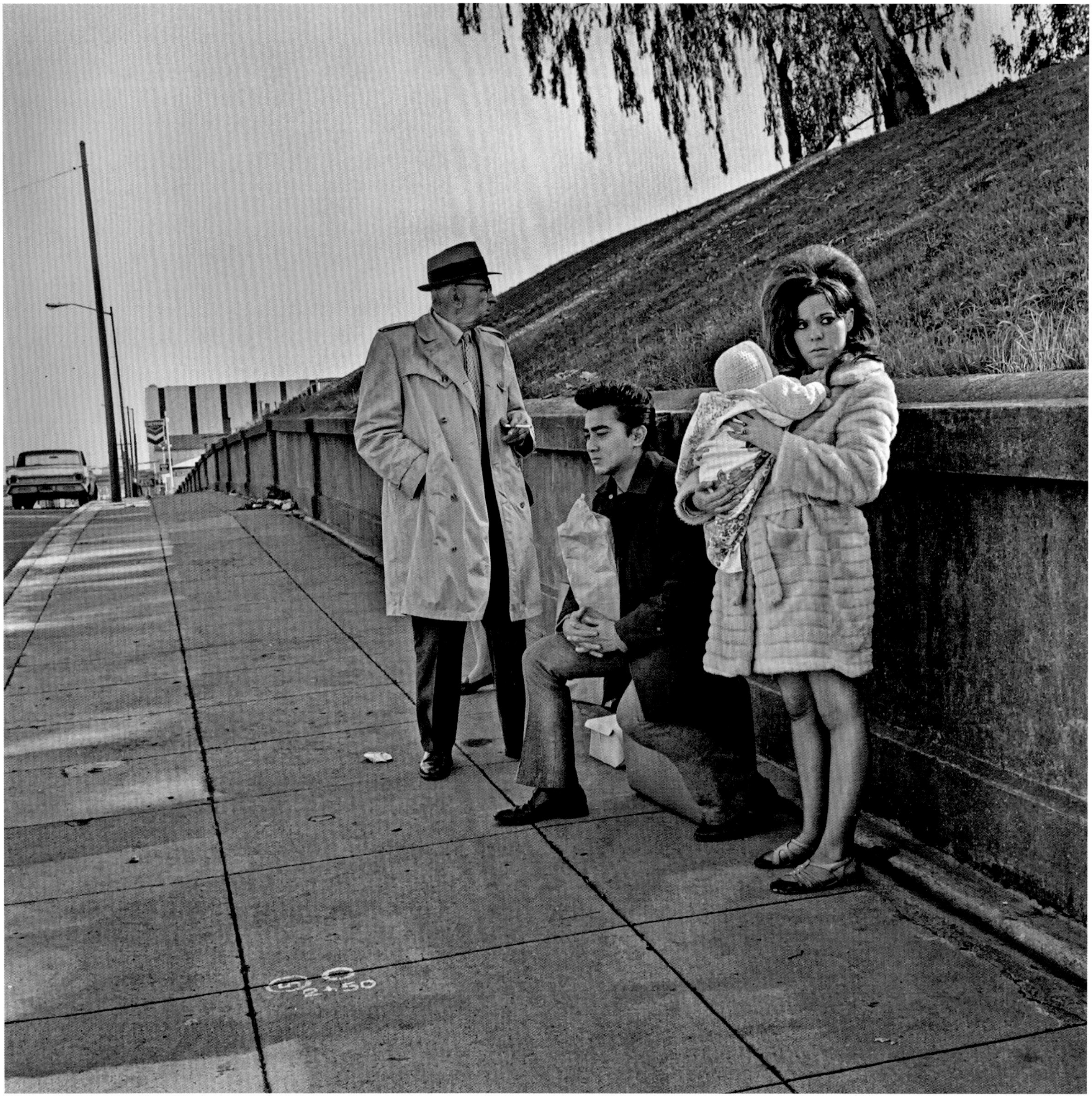

Couple with Baby, Sixteenth Street Bus Stop

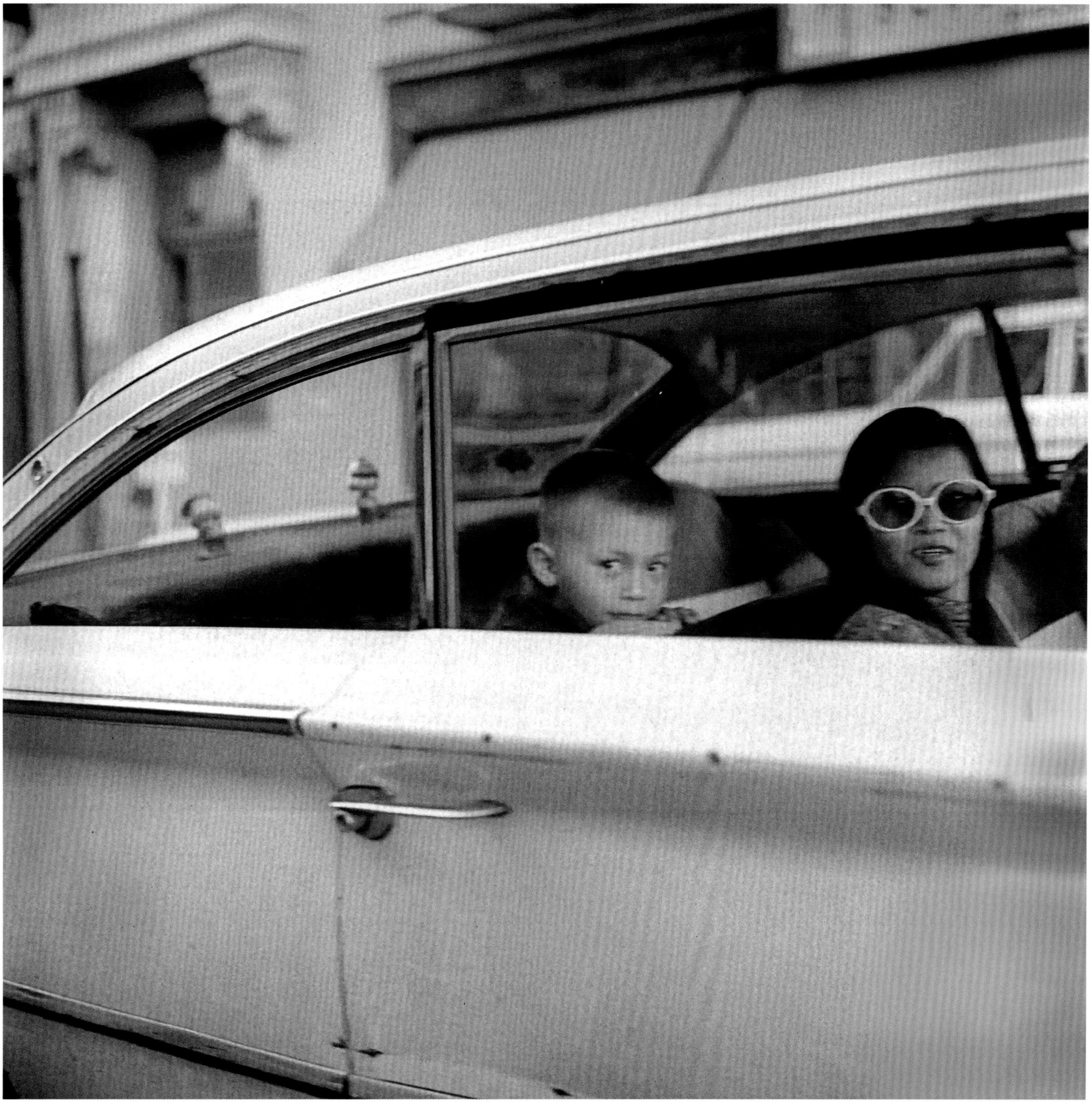

Mother and Son in the Car

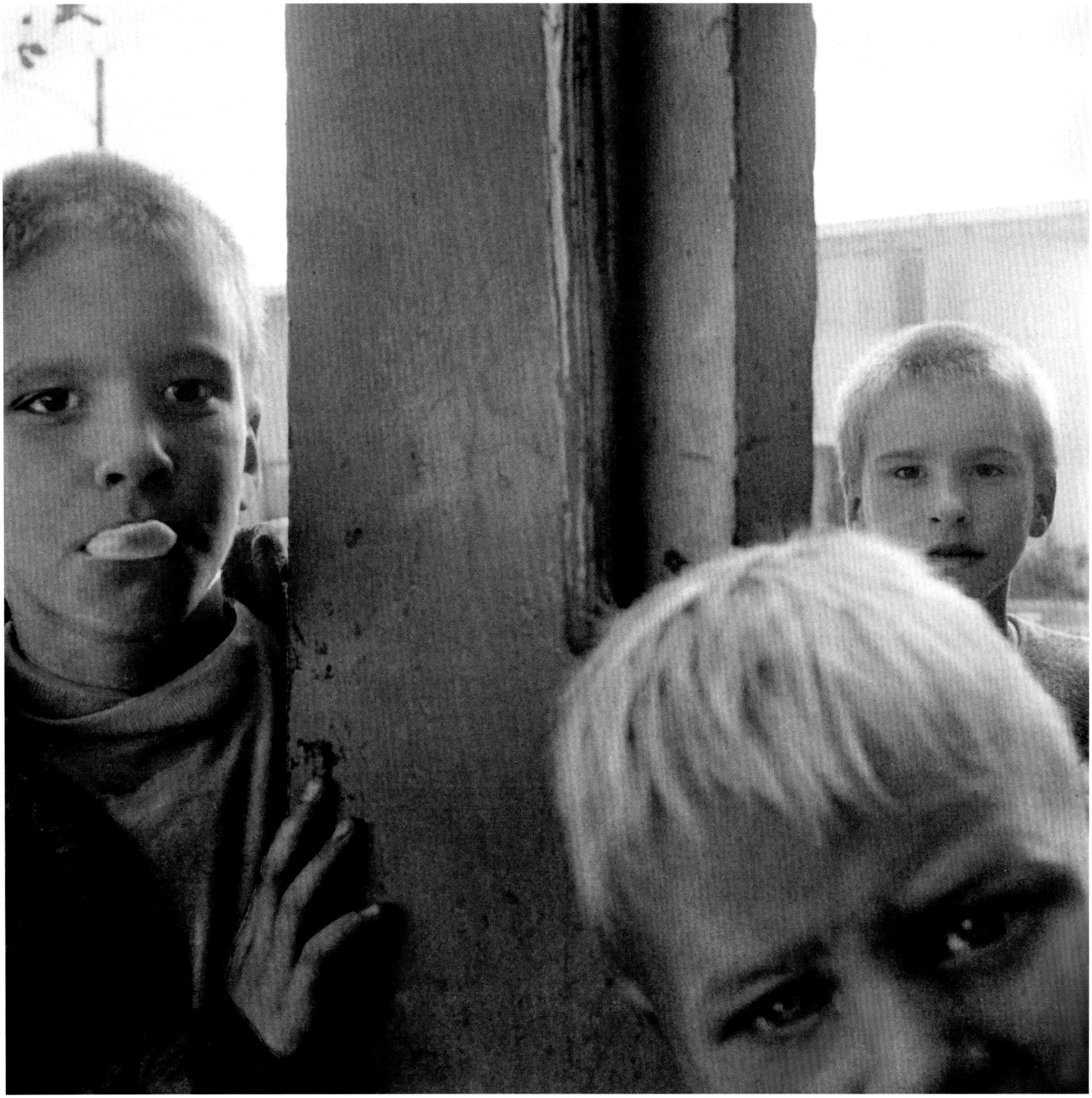

Boys and Bubble Gum, Los Angeles

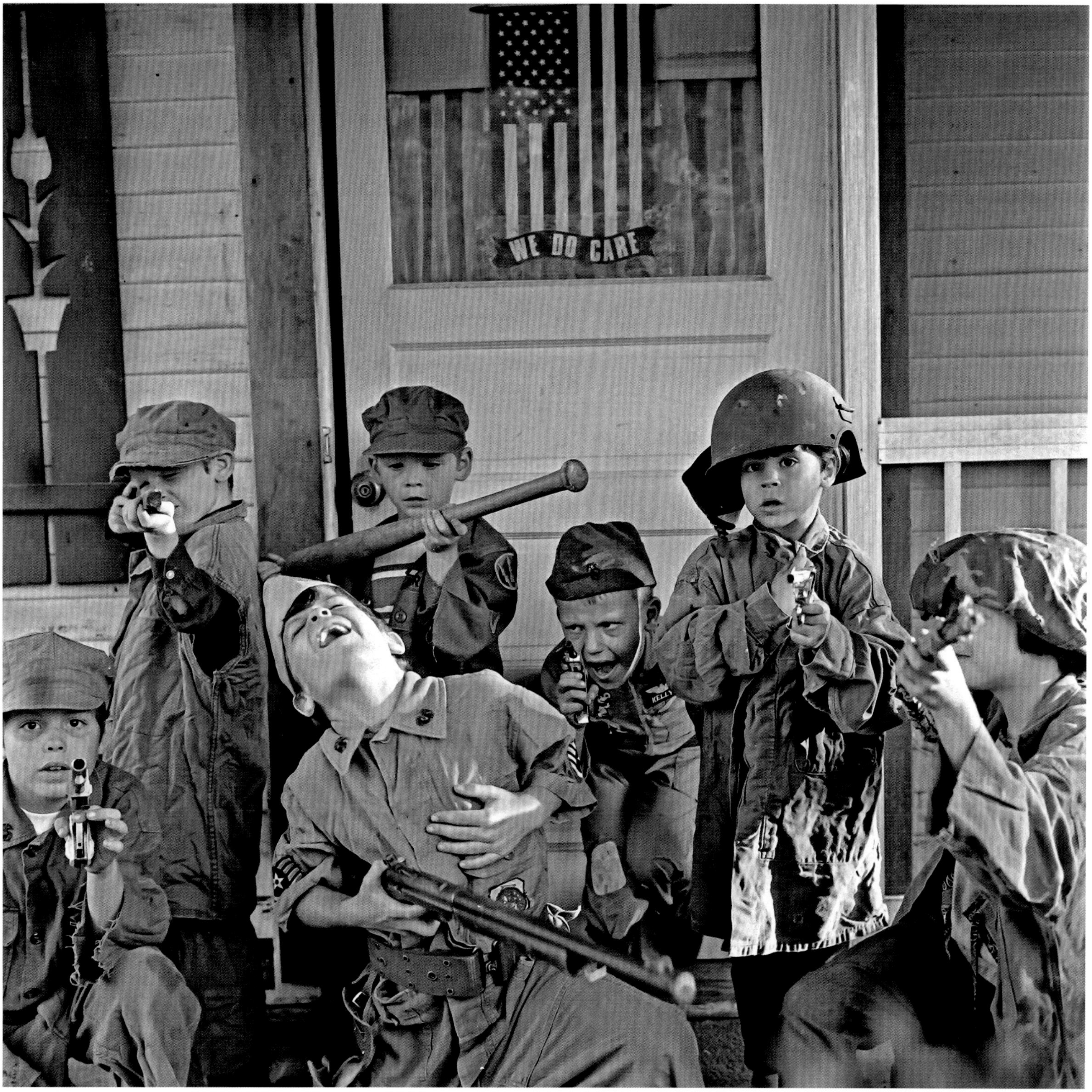

We Do Care, Venice, California

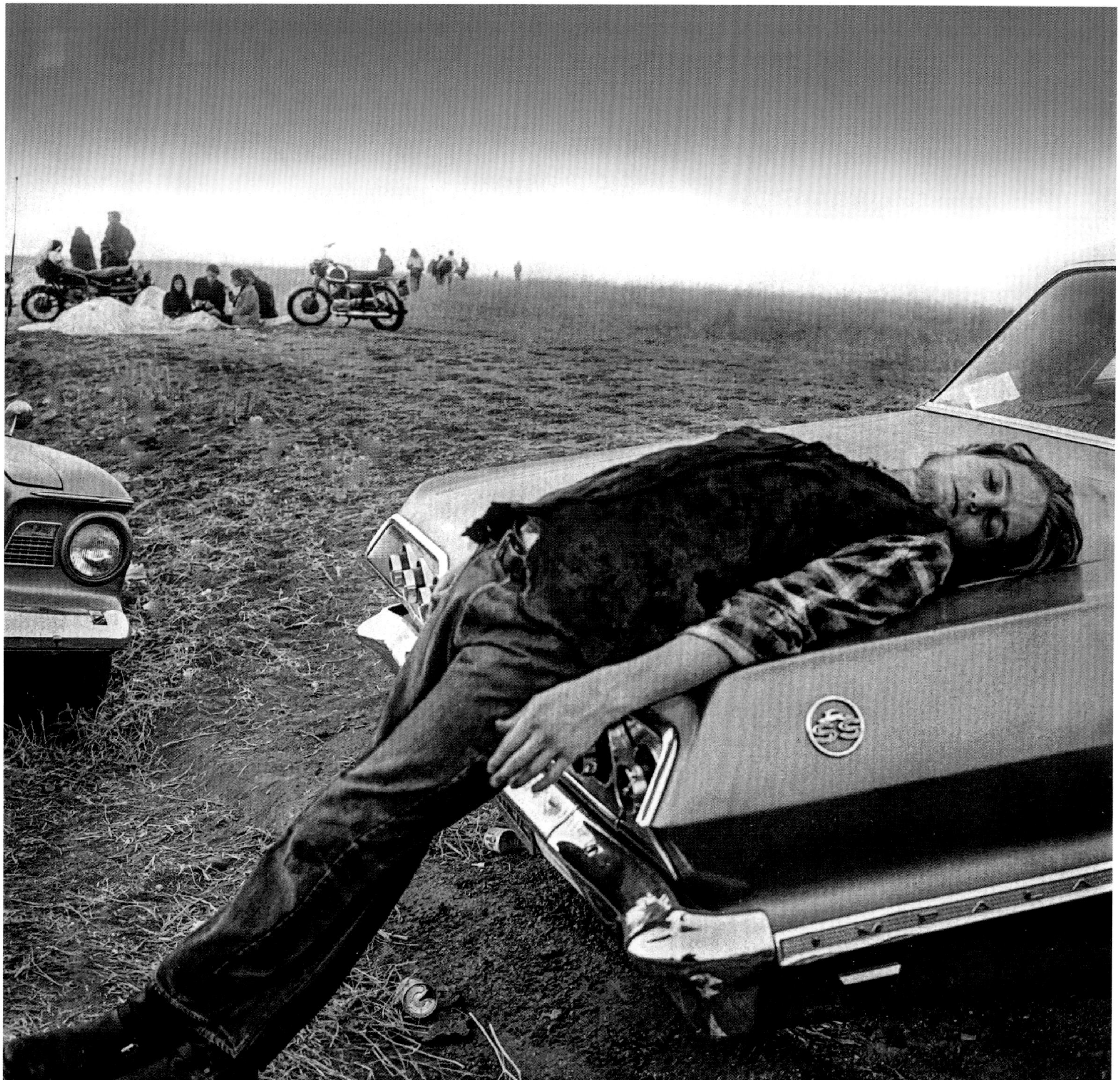

Man Sleeping at Altamont

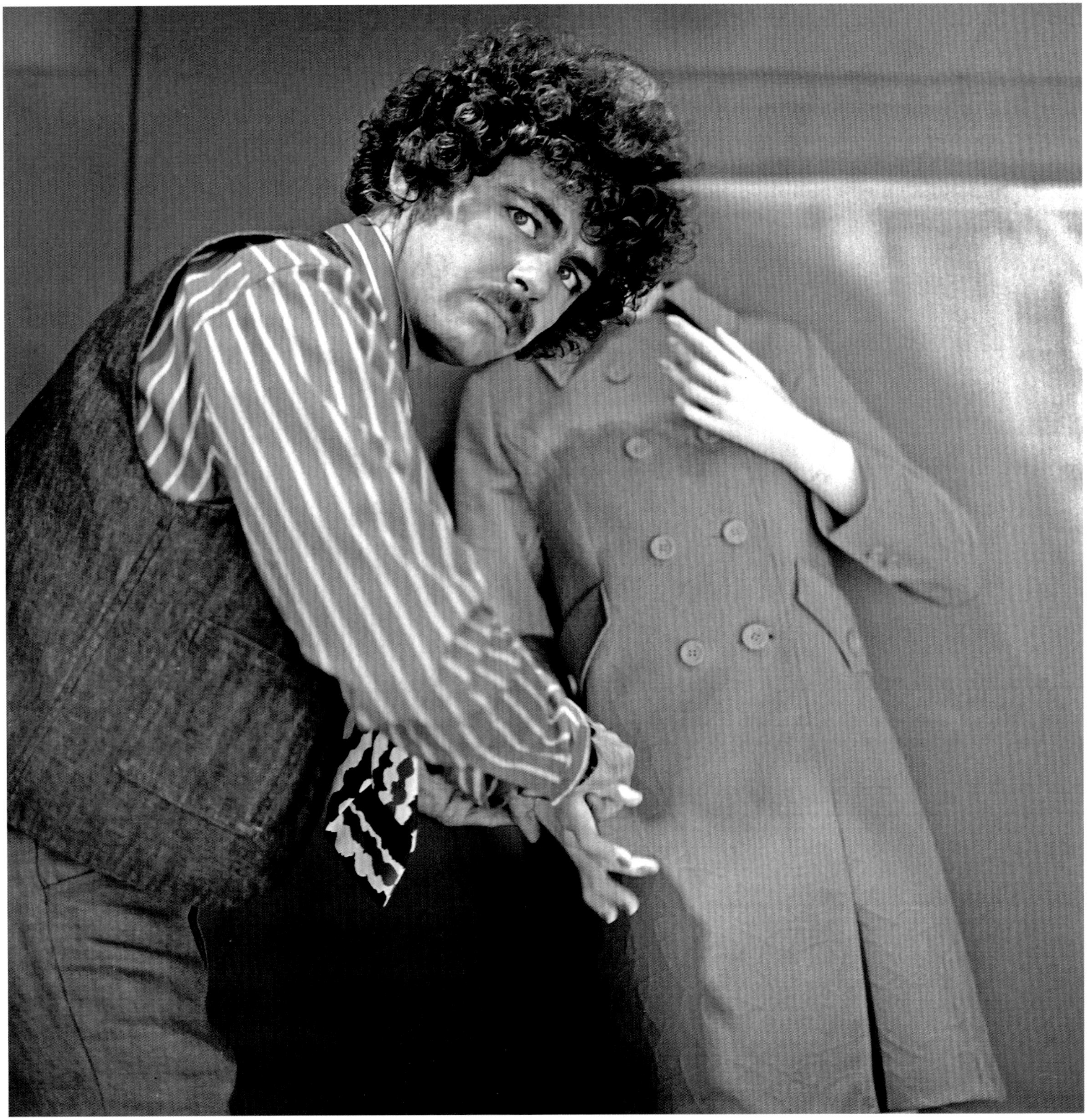

Window Dresser, Macy's Union Square

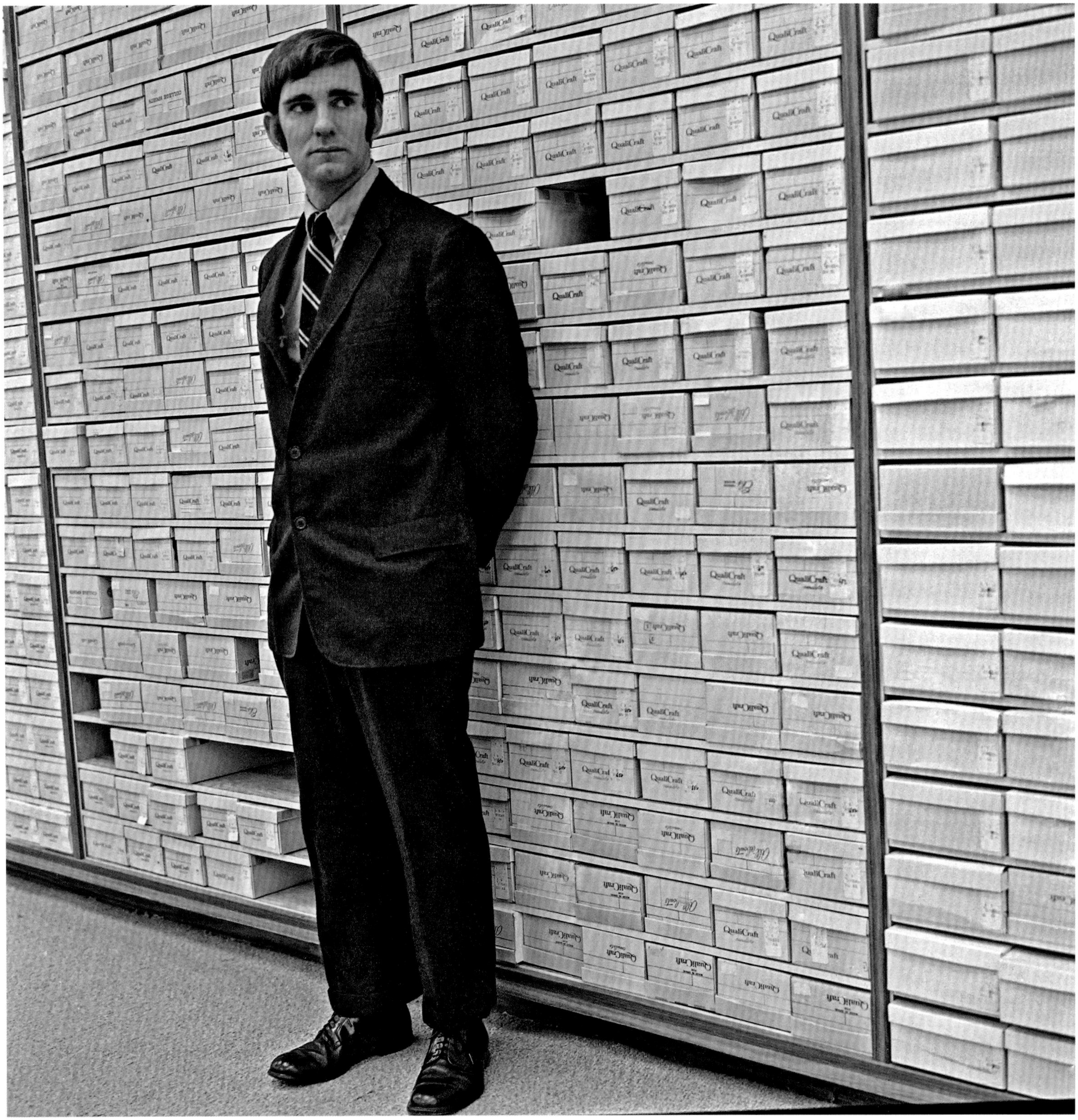

Shoe Salesman

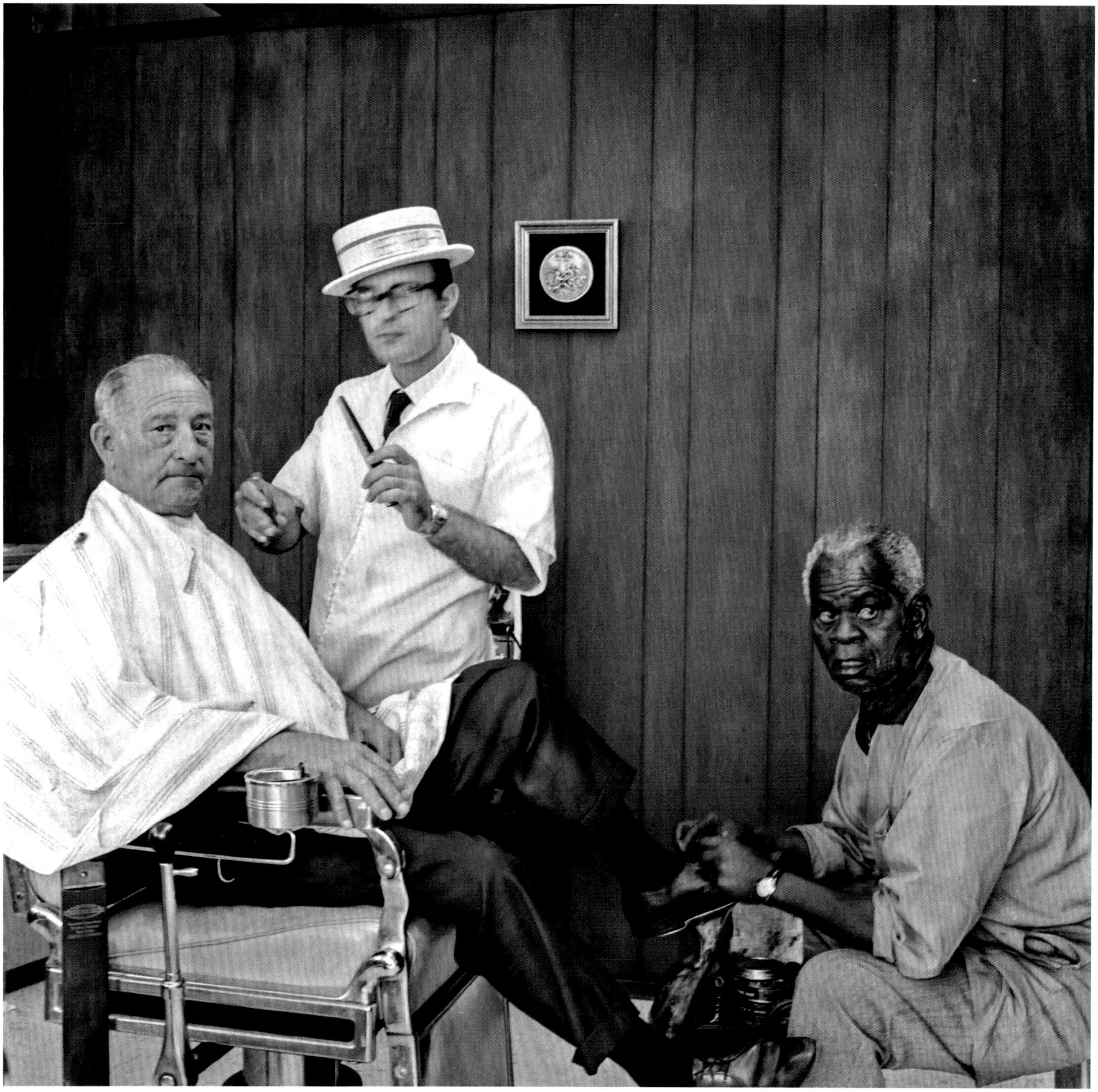

Haircut and Shoeshine

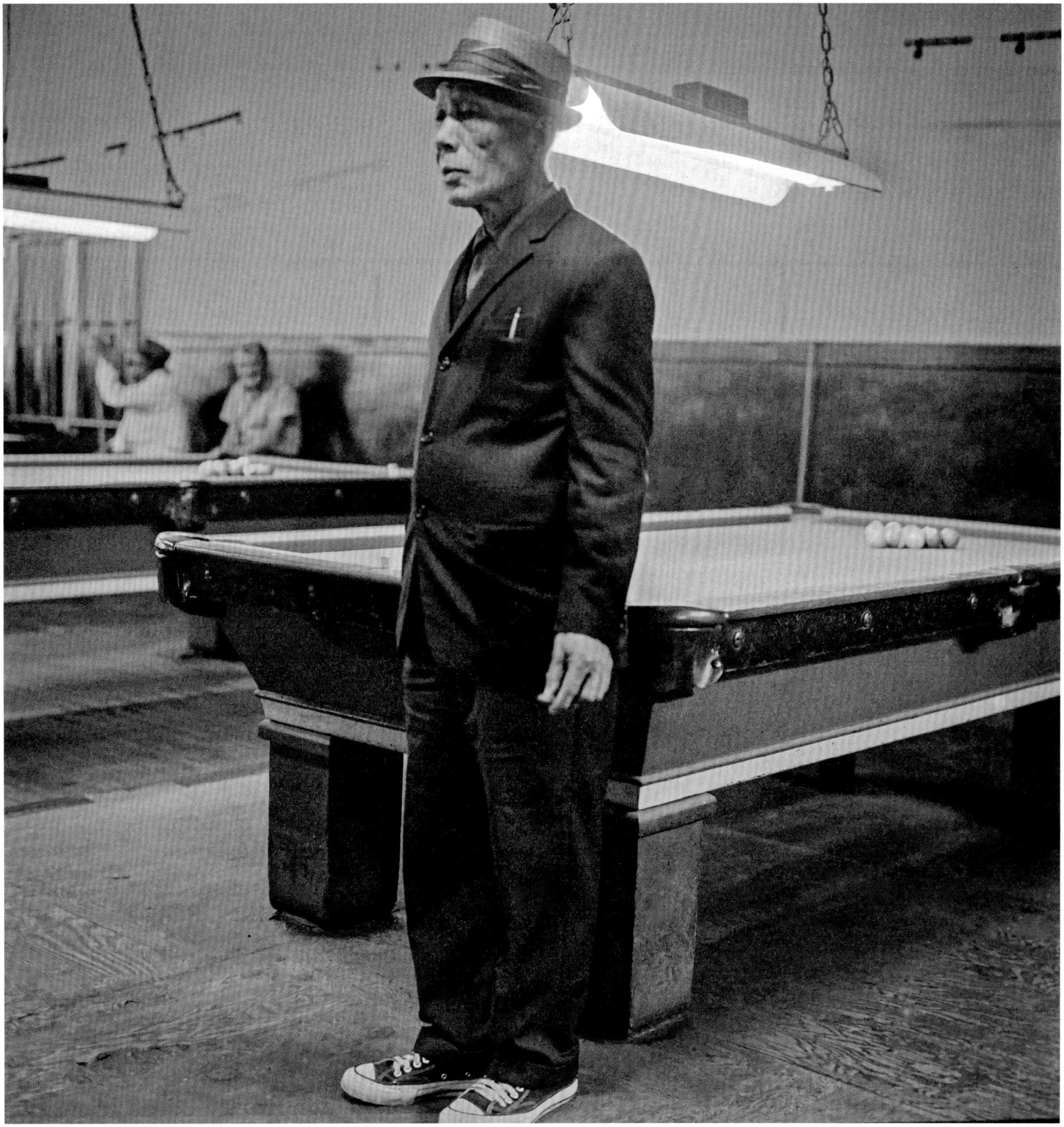

Manilatown Pool Hall, Kearny and Jackson Streets

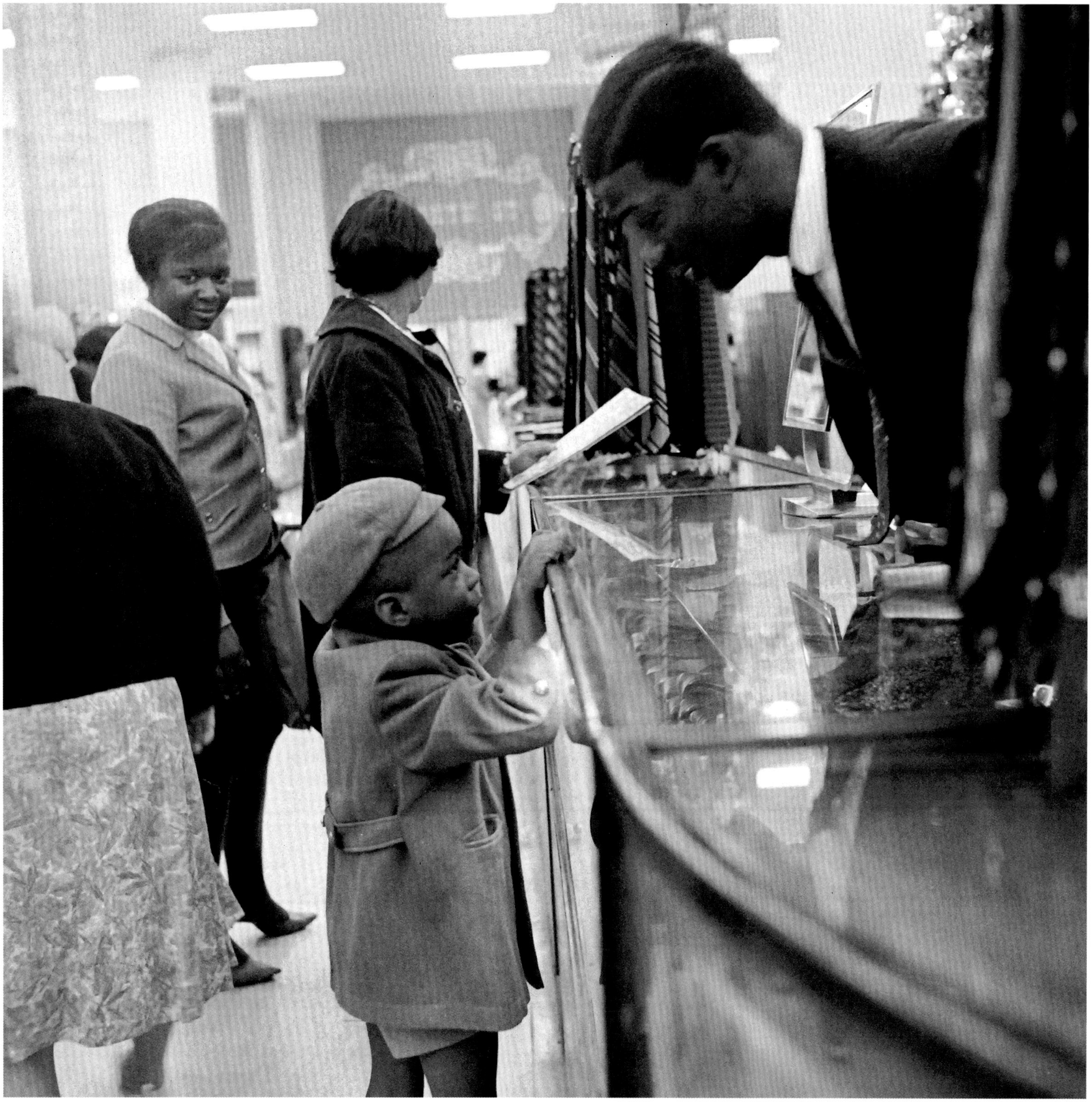

Boy and Salesman at Emporium Counter, Market Street

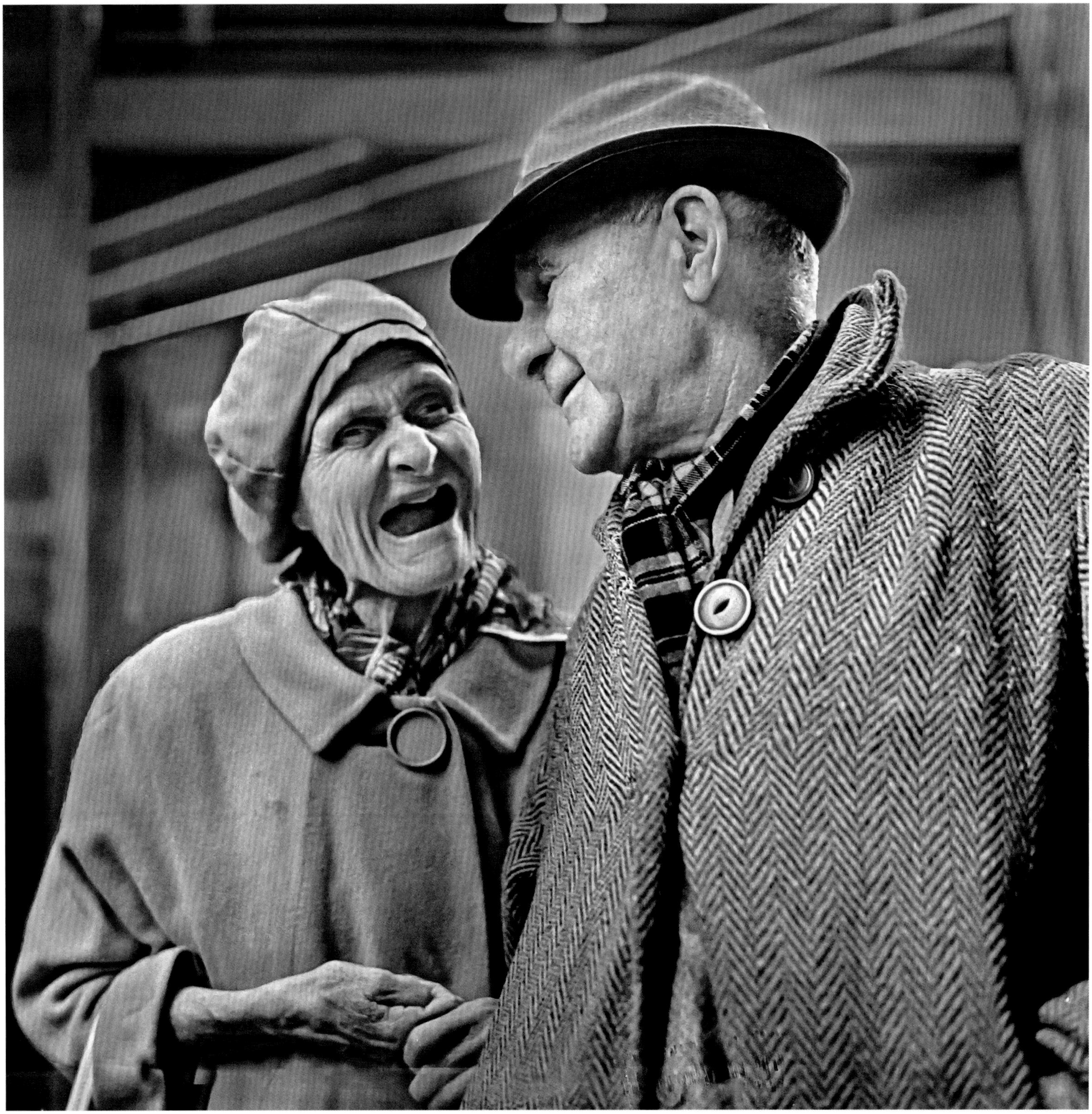

Loving Couple, Downtown

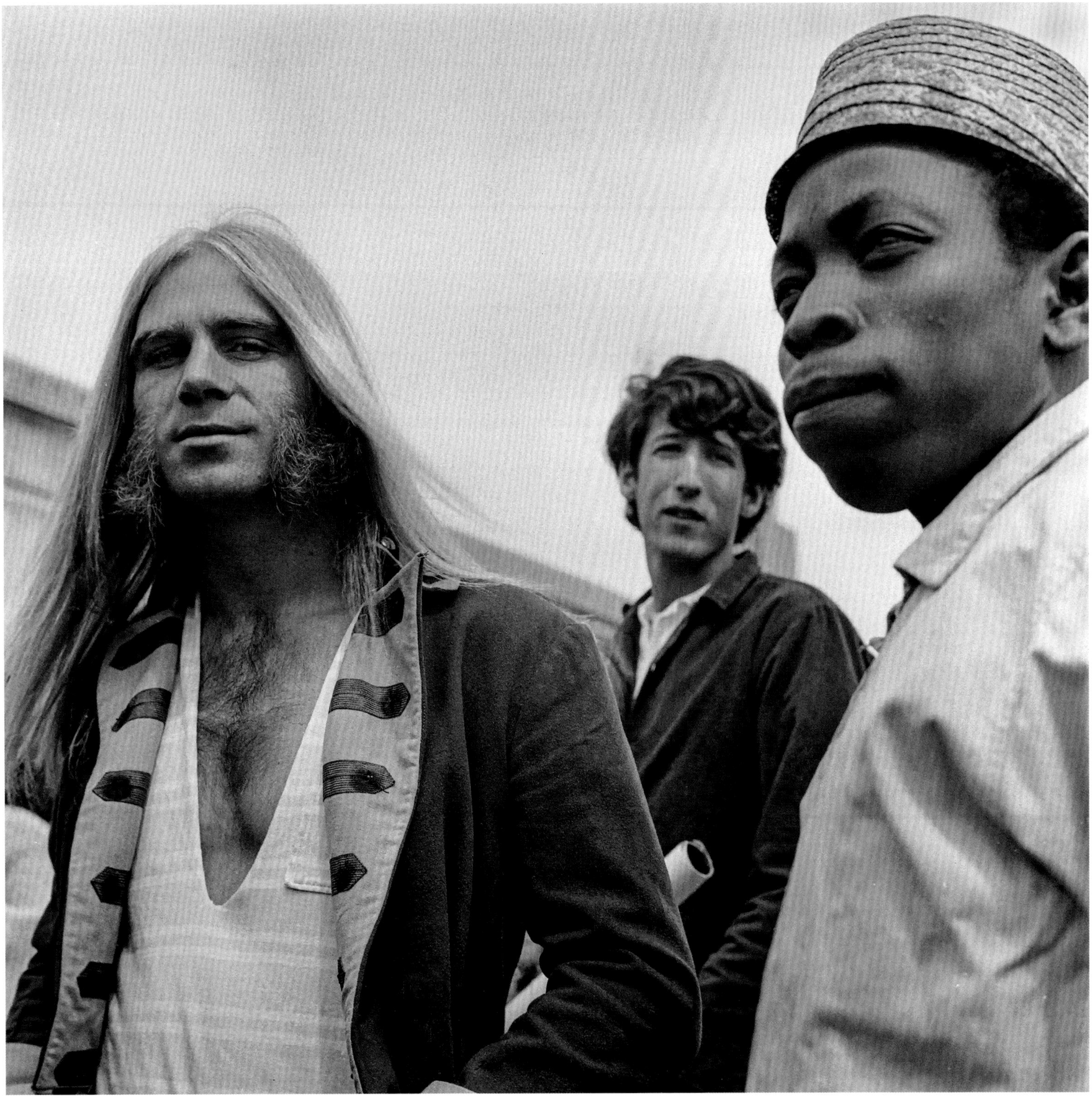

Mutton Chops and Beanie, Peace Rally

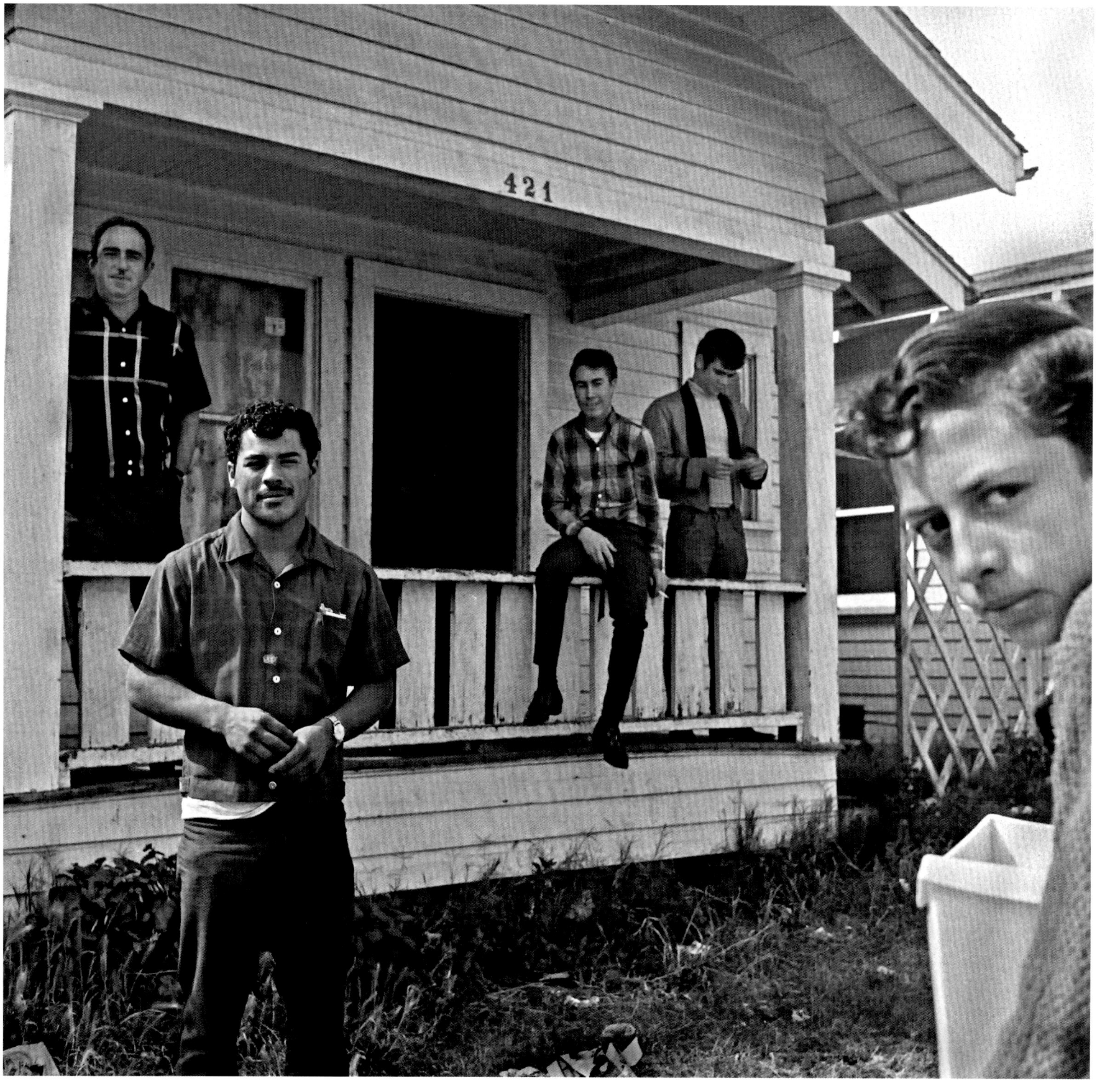

Men Waiting on Porch, Venice, California

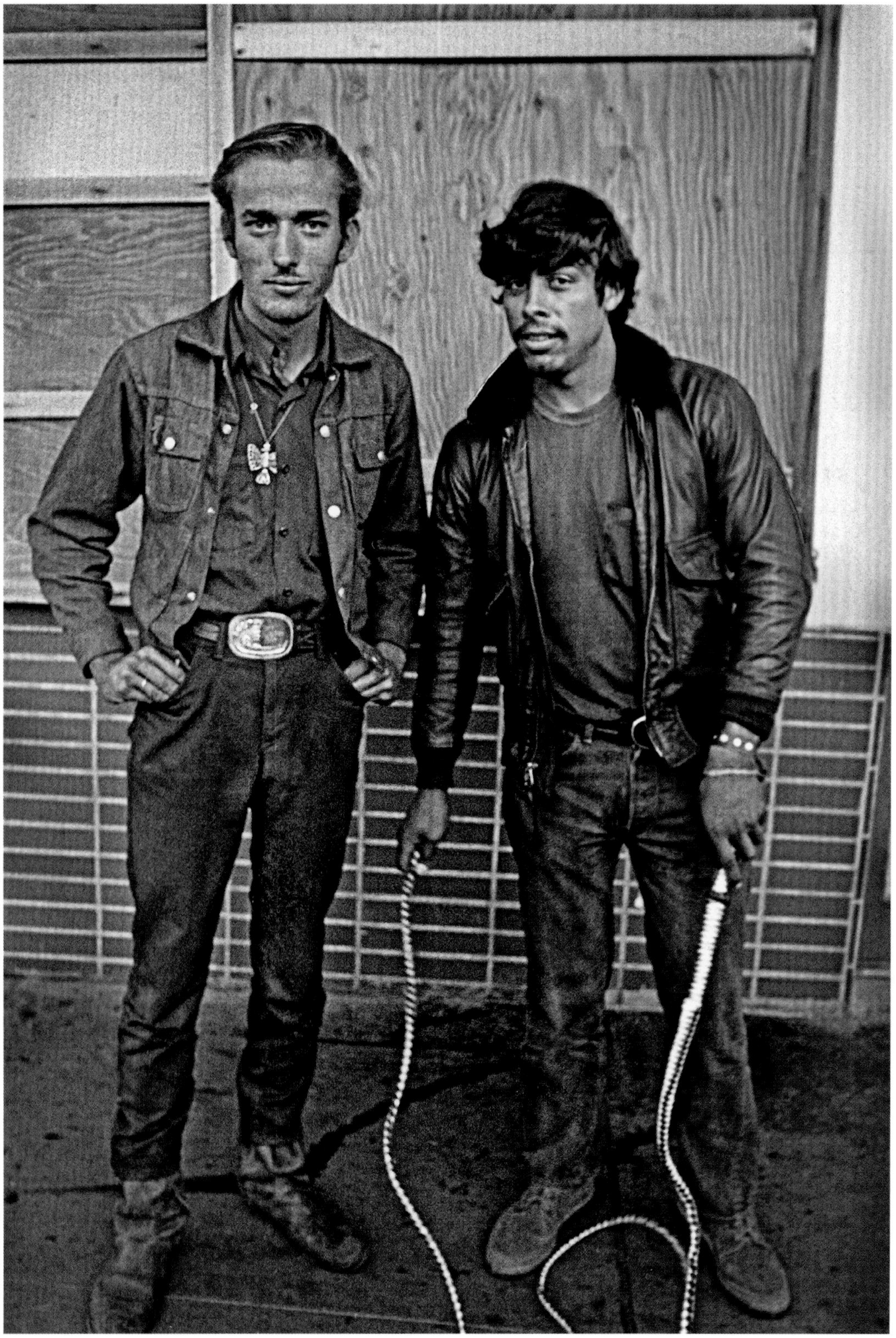

Carnies with Whips, Playland at the Beach

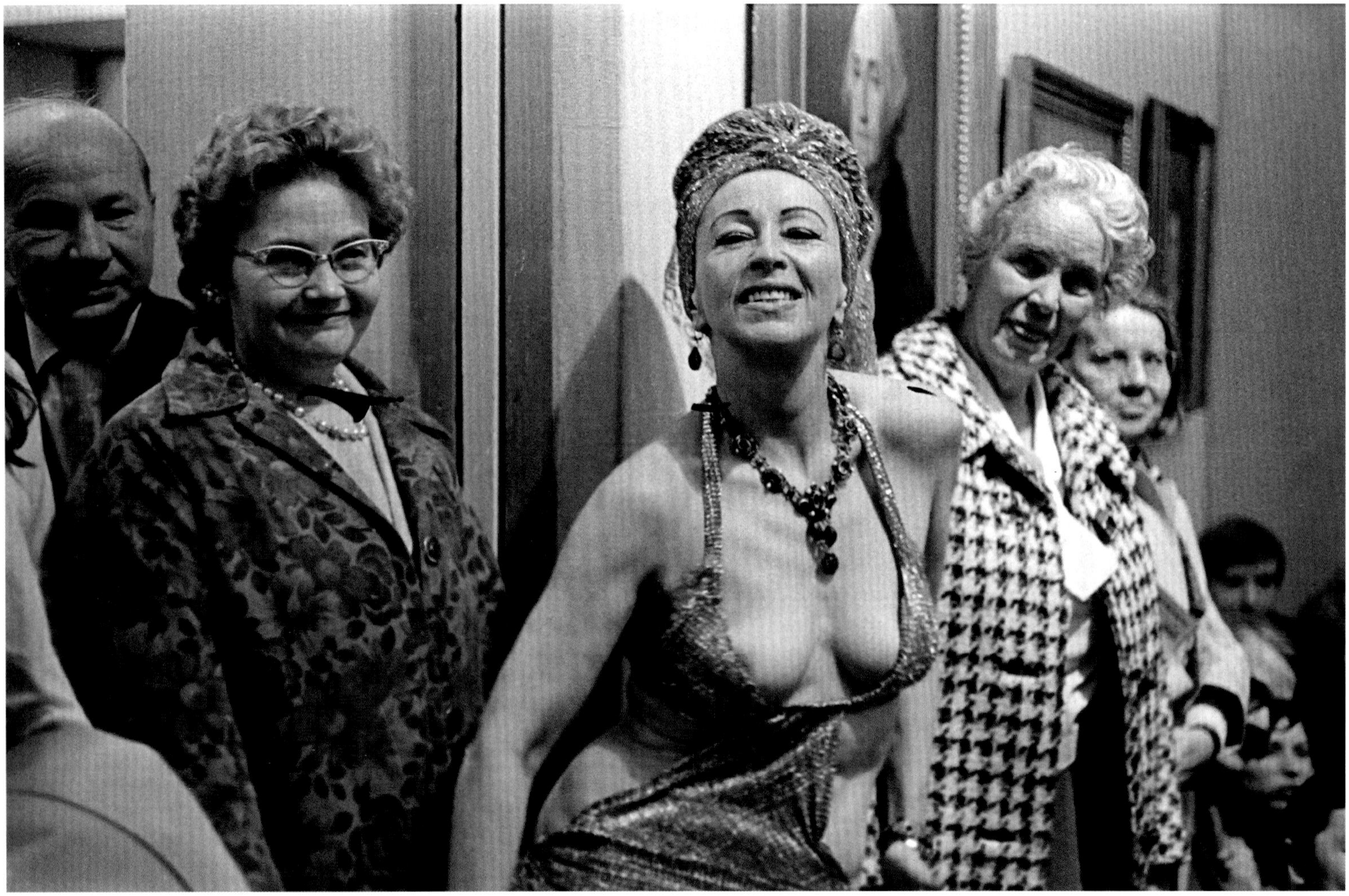

Art Opening at the de Young Museum

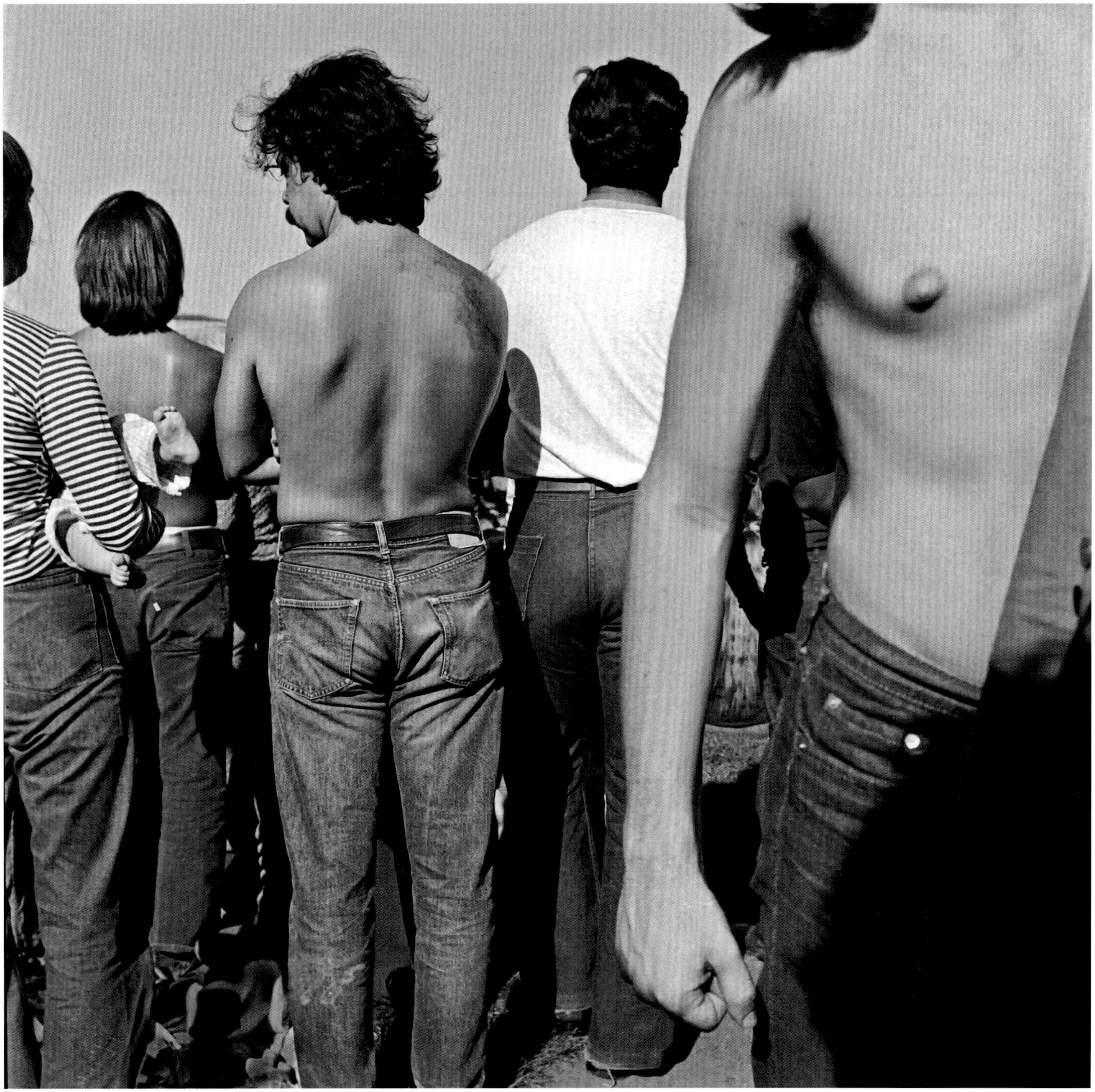

Shirtless Men and Baby Feet, Los Angeles

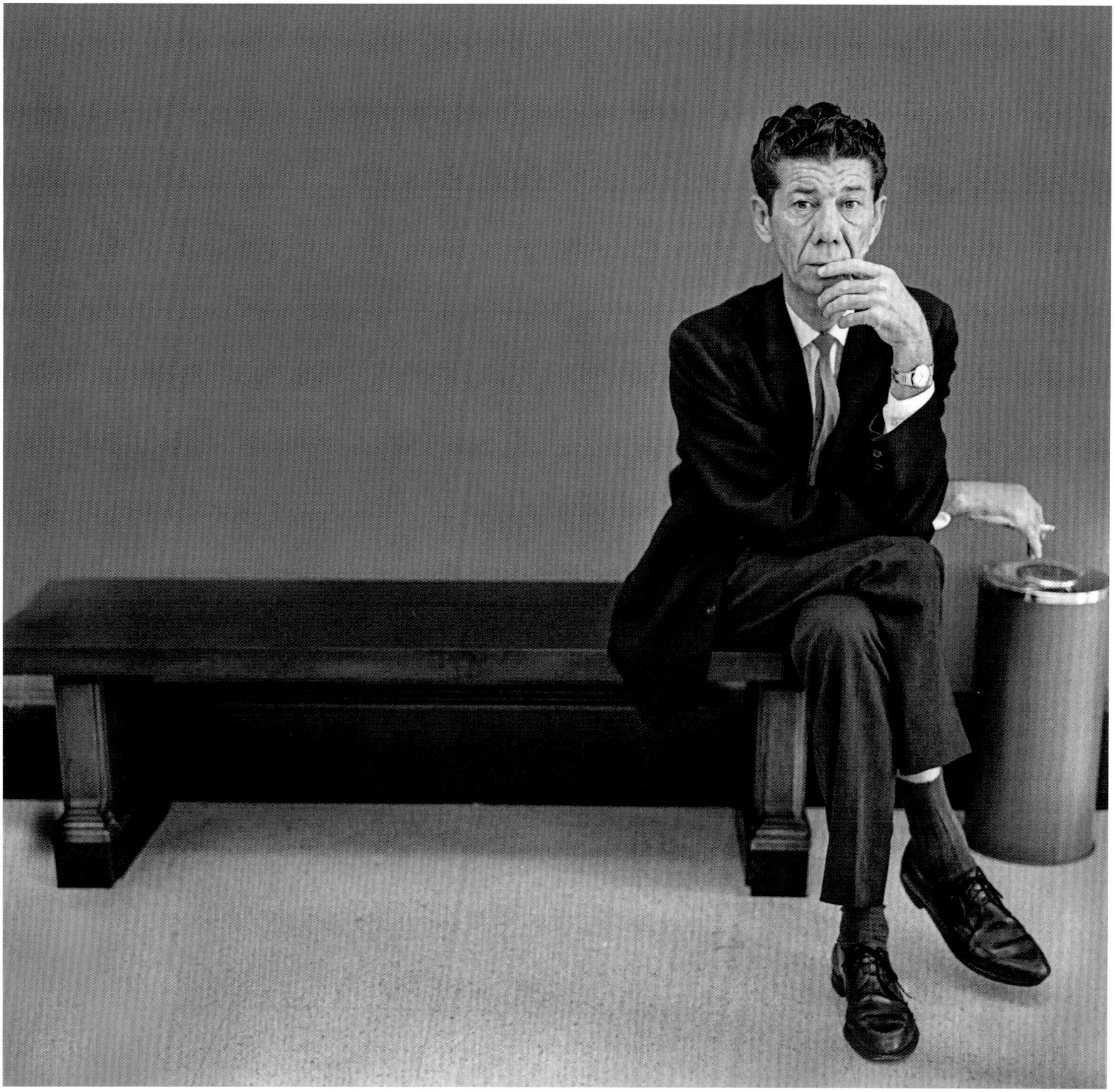

Man Smoking in Lobby

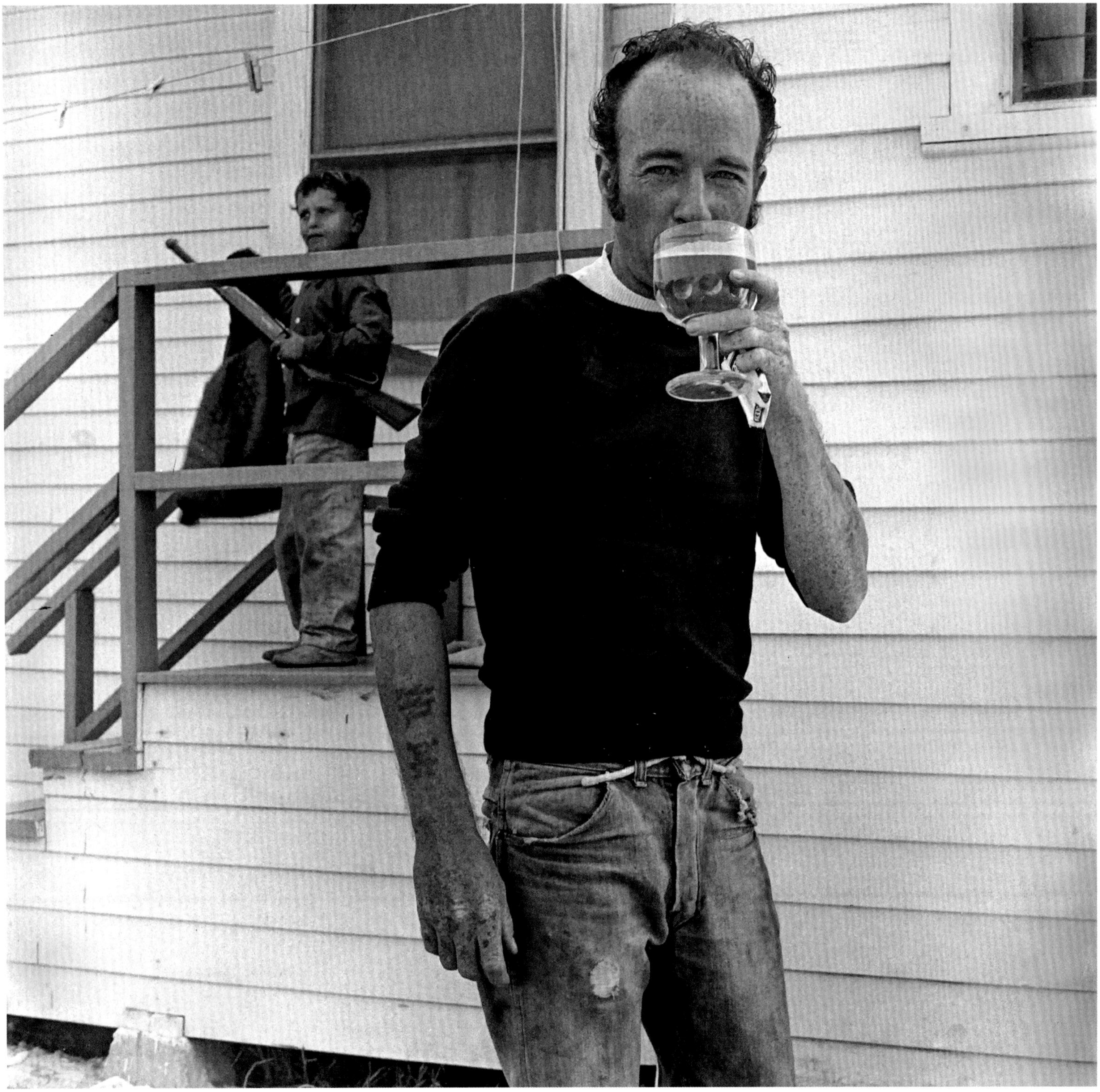

Father and Son and Beer and Gun, Venice, California

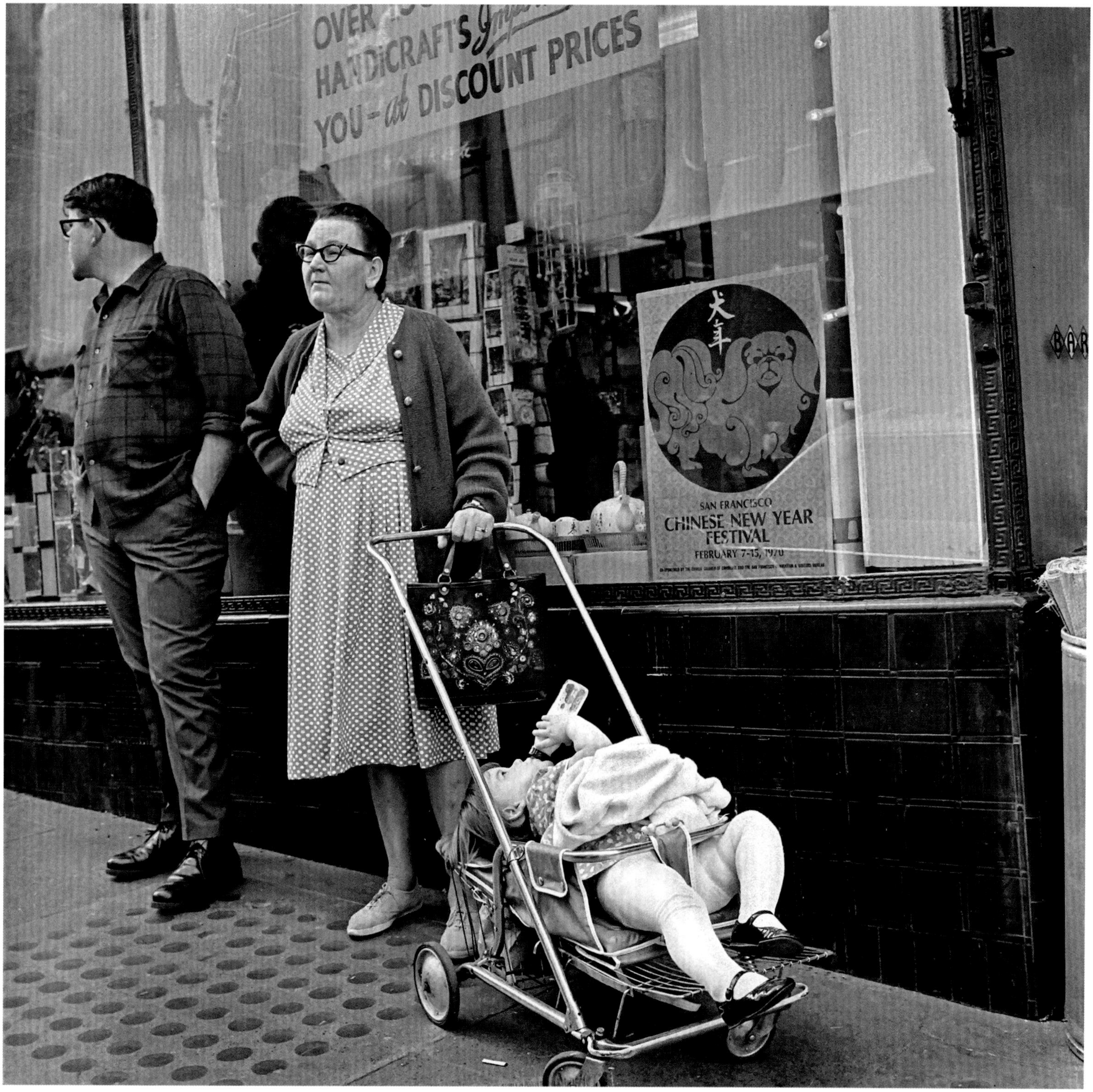

Grandmother and Baby Girl, Chinatown

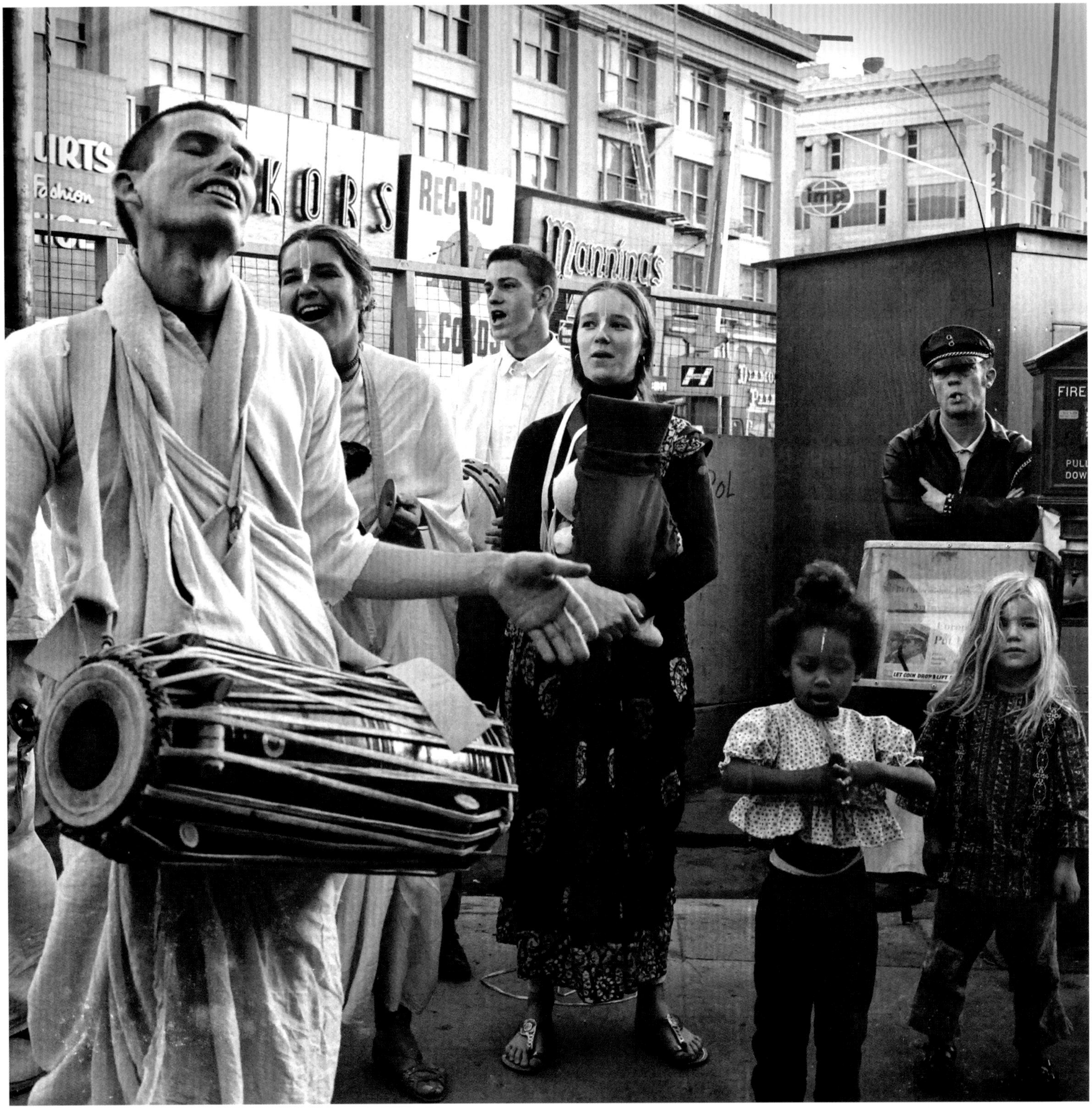

Hare Krishnas and Man in Leather, Market Street

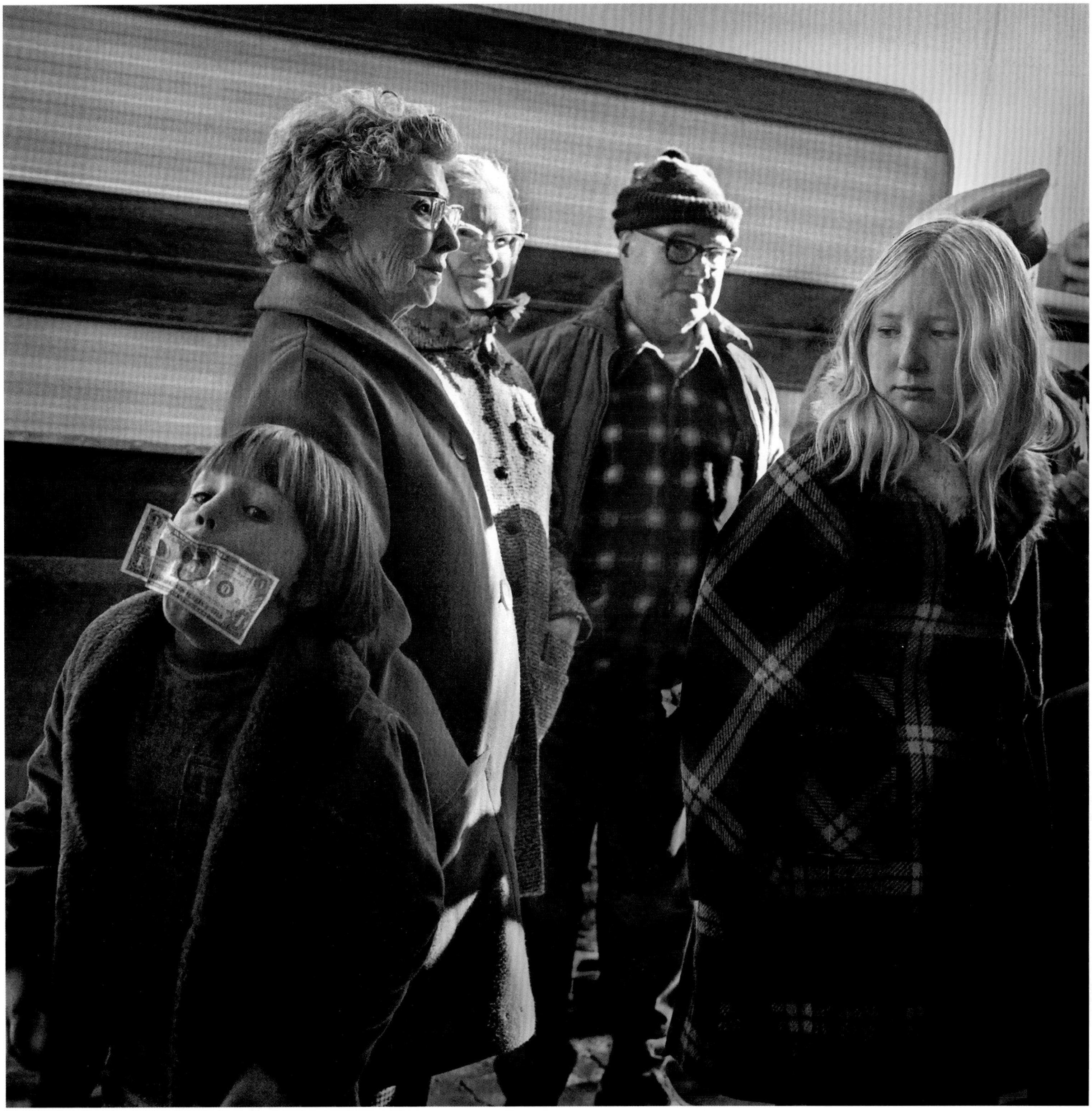

Girl with Dollar Bill

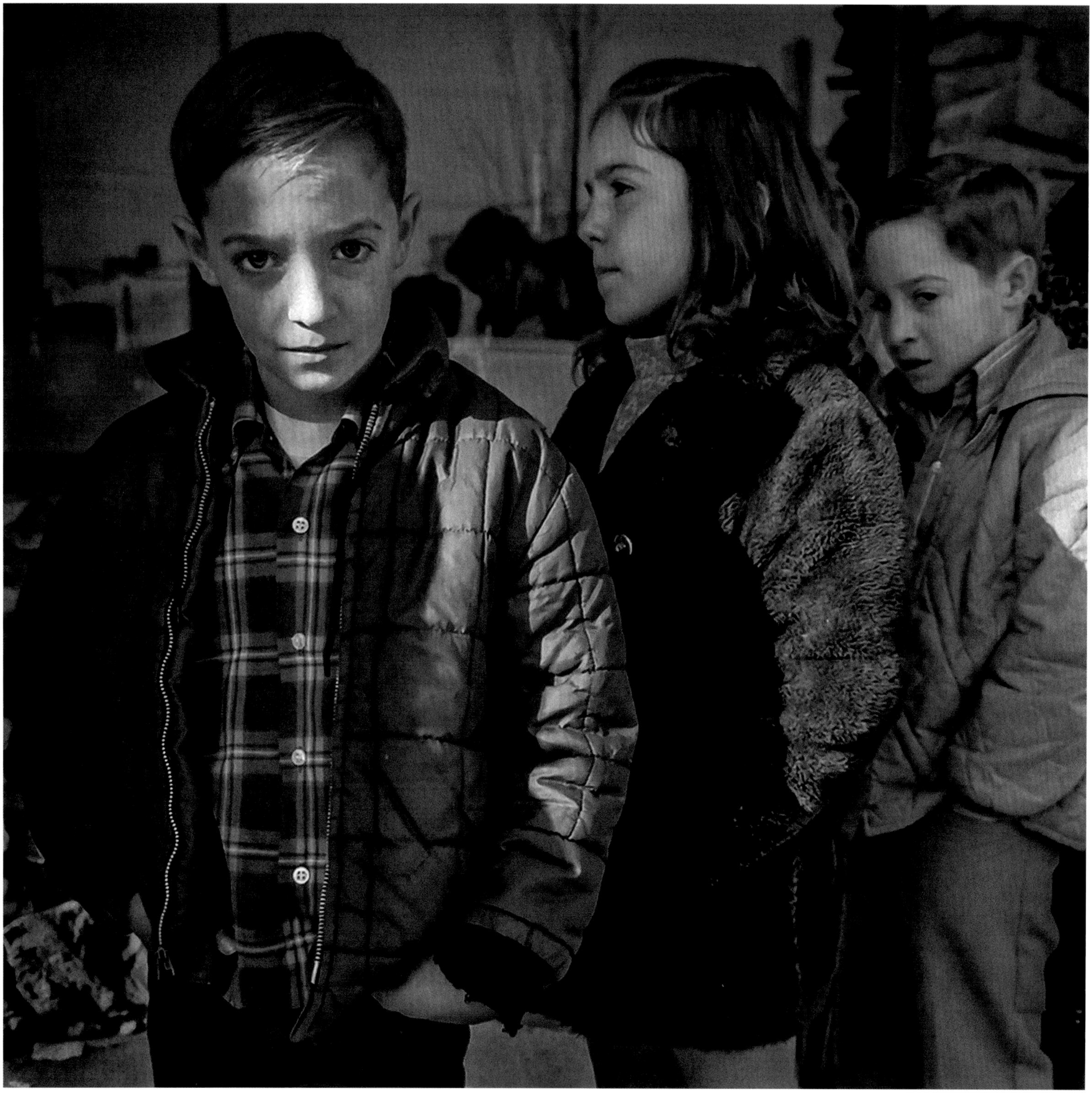

Boy and Siblings

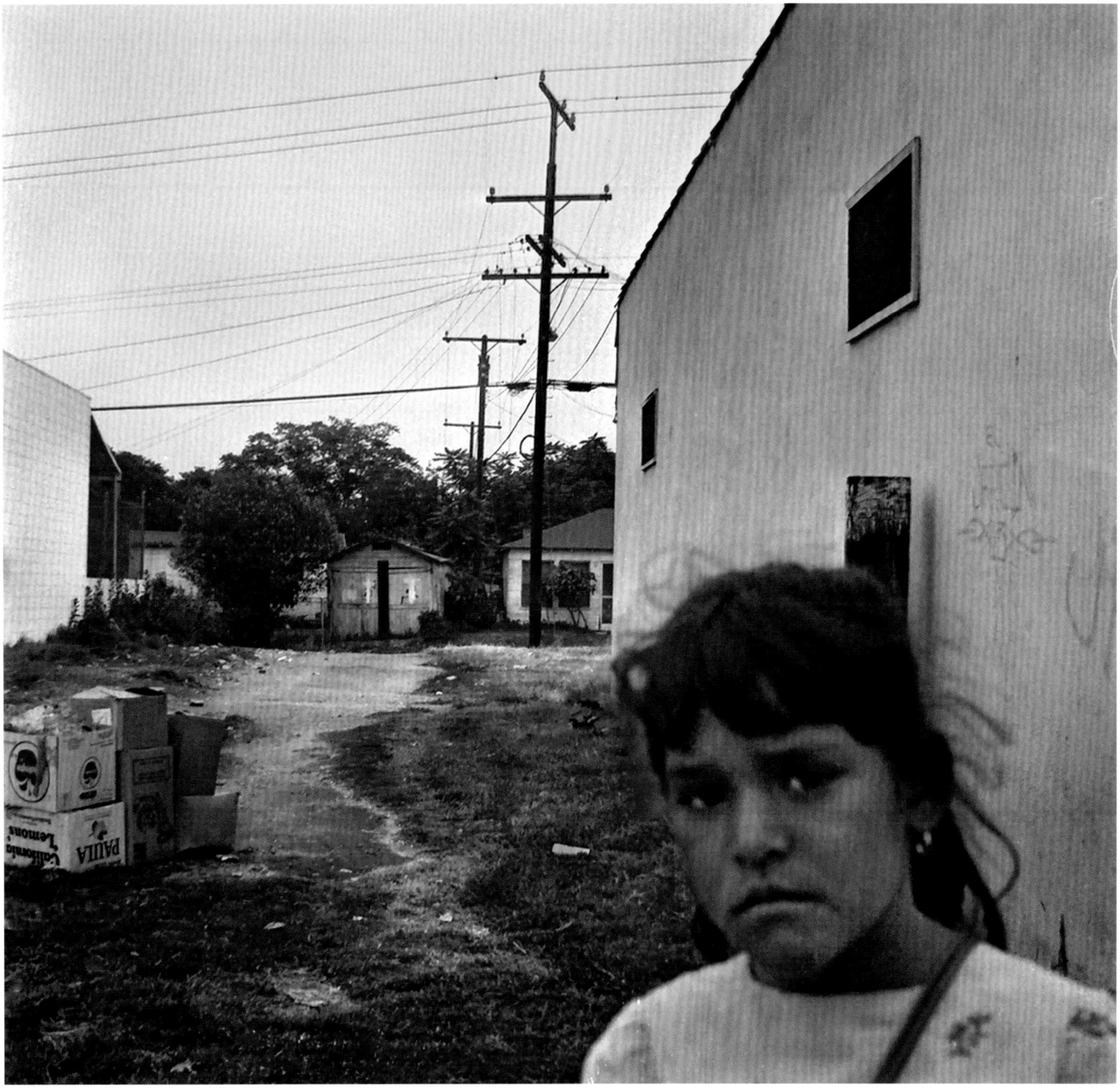

Girl in Alley, Venice, California

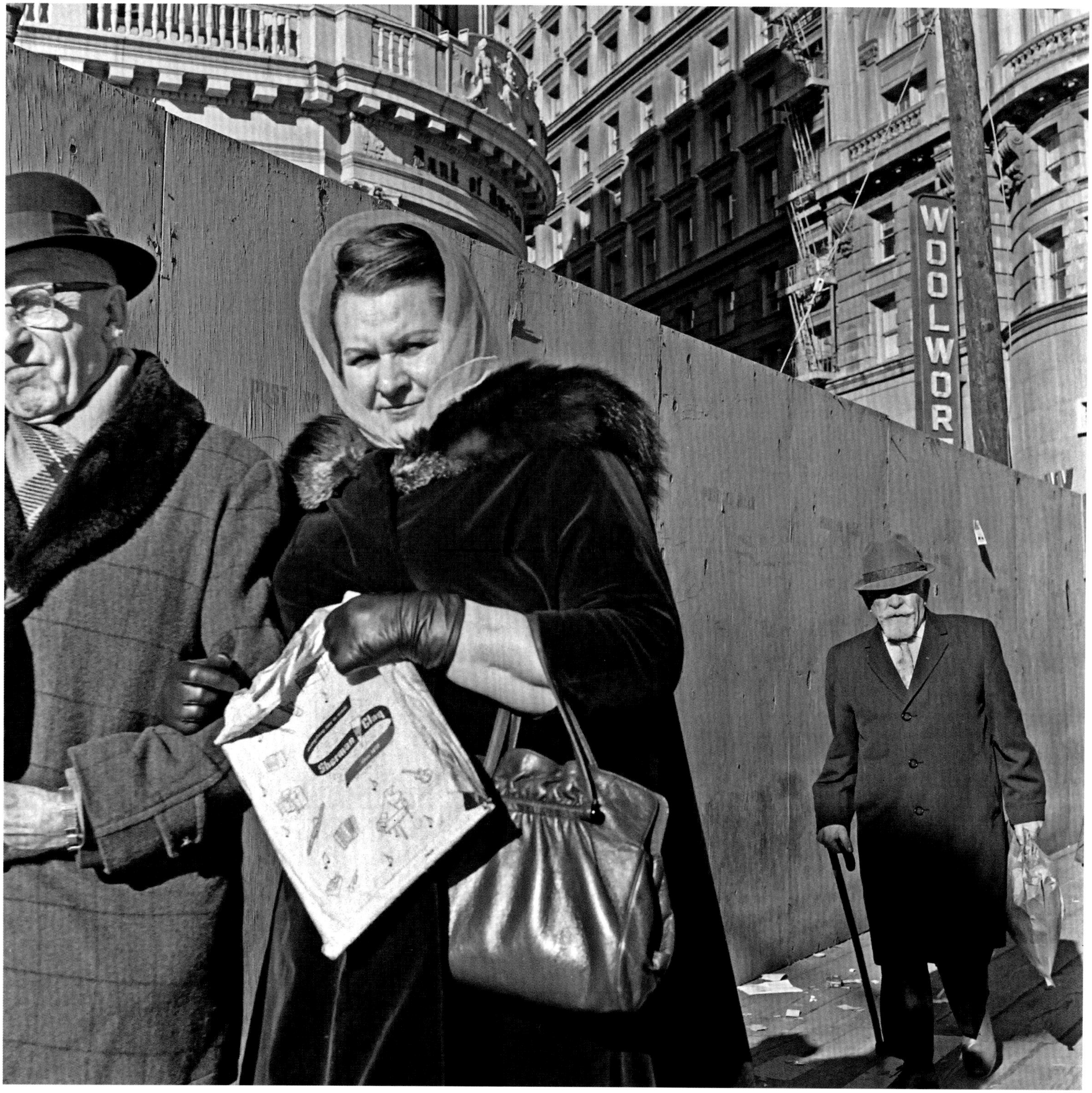

Couple Passing BART Station Construction, Market Street near Powell

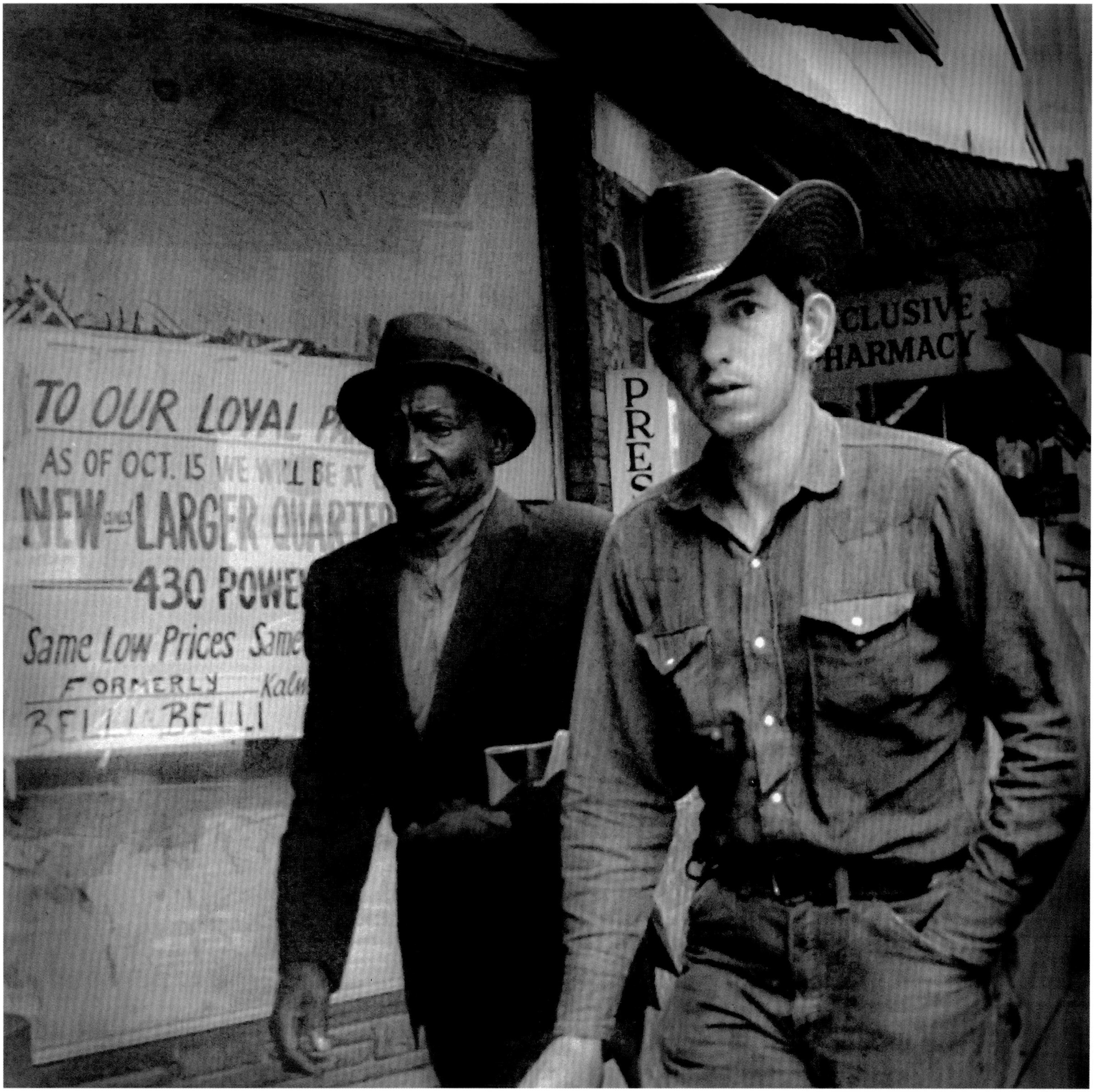

Two Men Walking on Powell Street

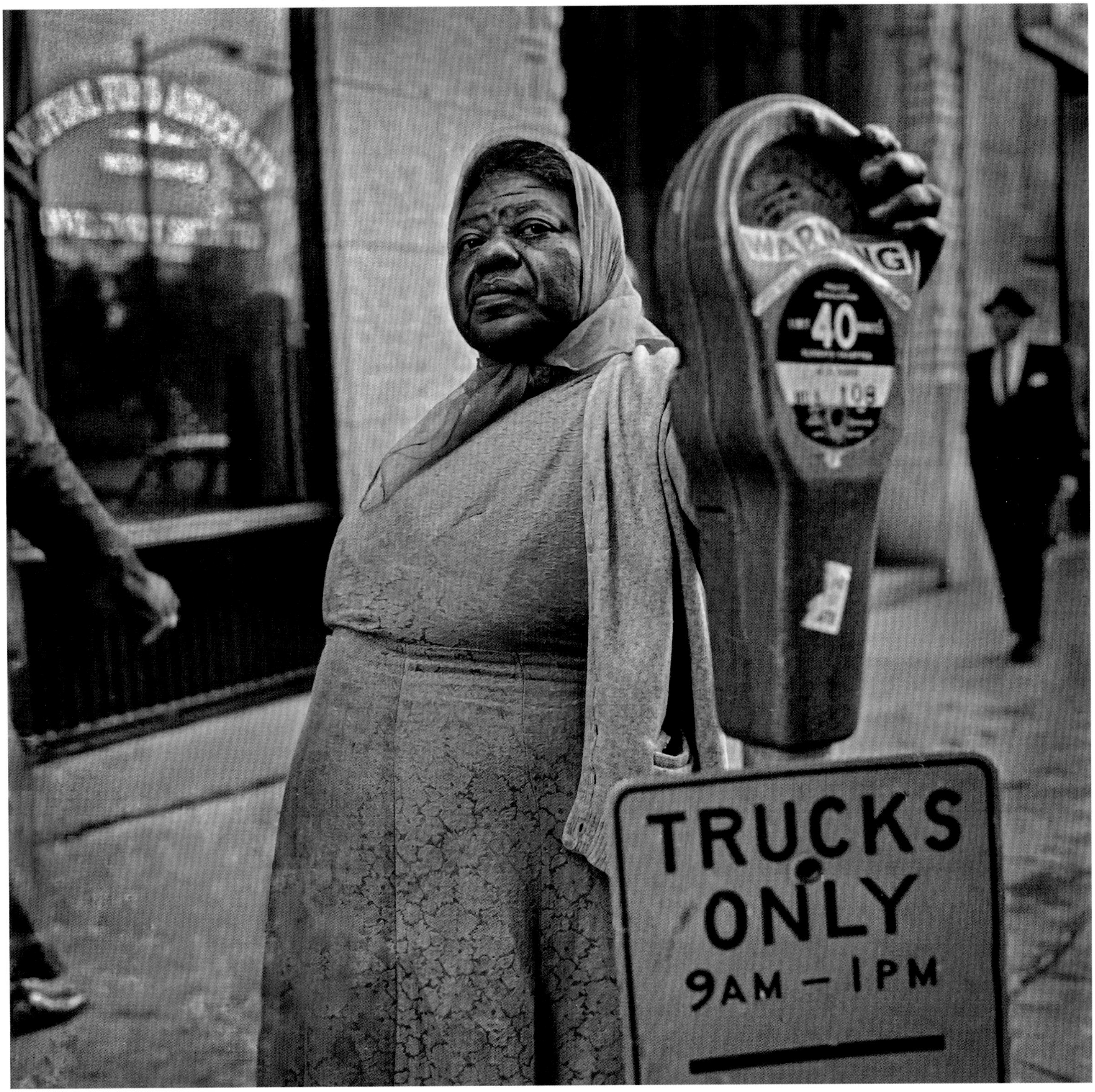

Woman and Parking Meter, Downtown

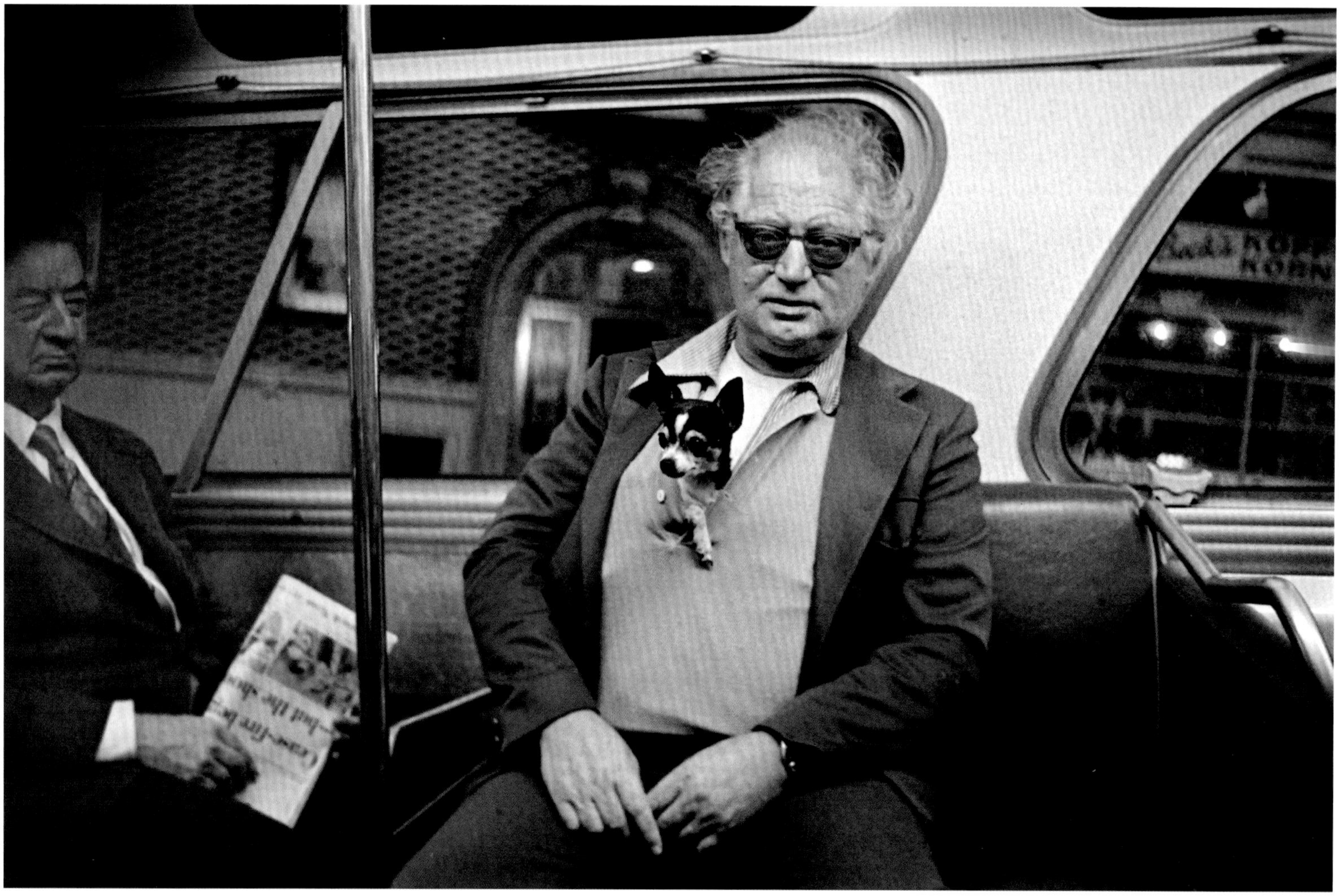

Man on MUNI with Chihuahua

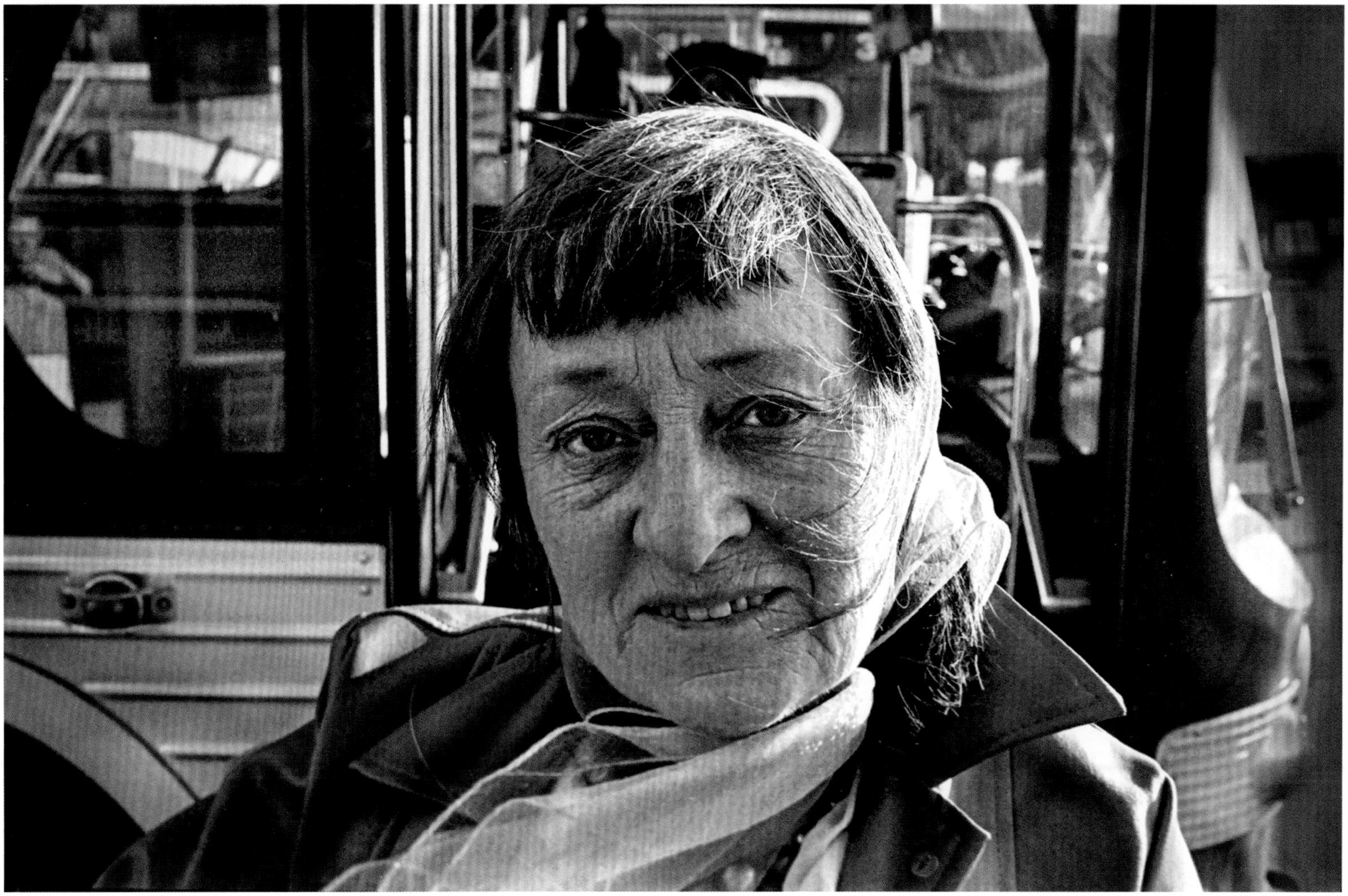

Woman with Scarf and Bus

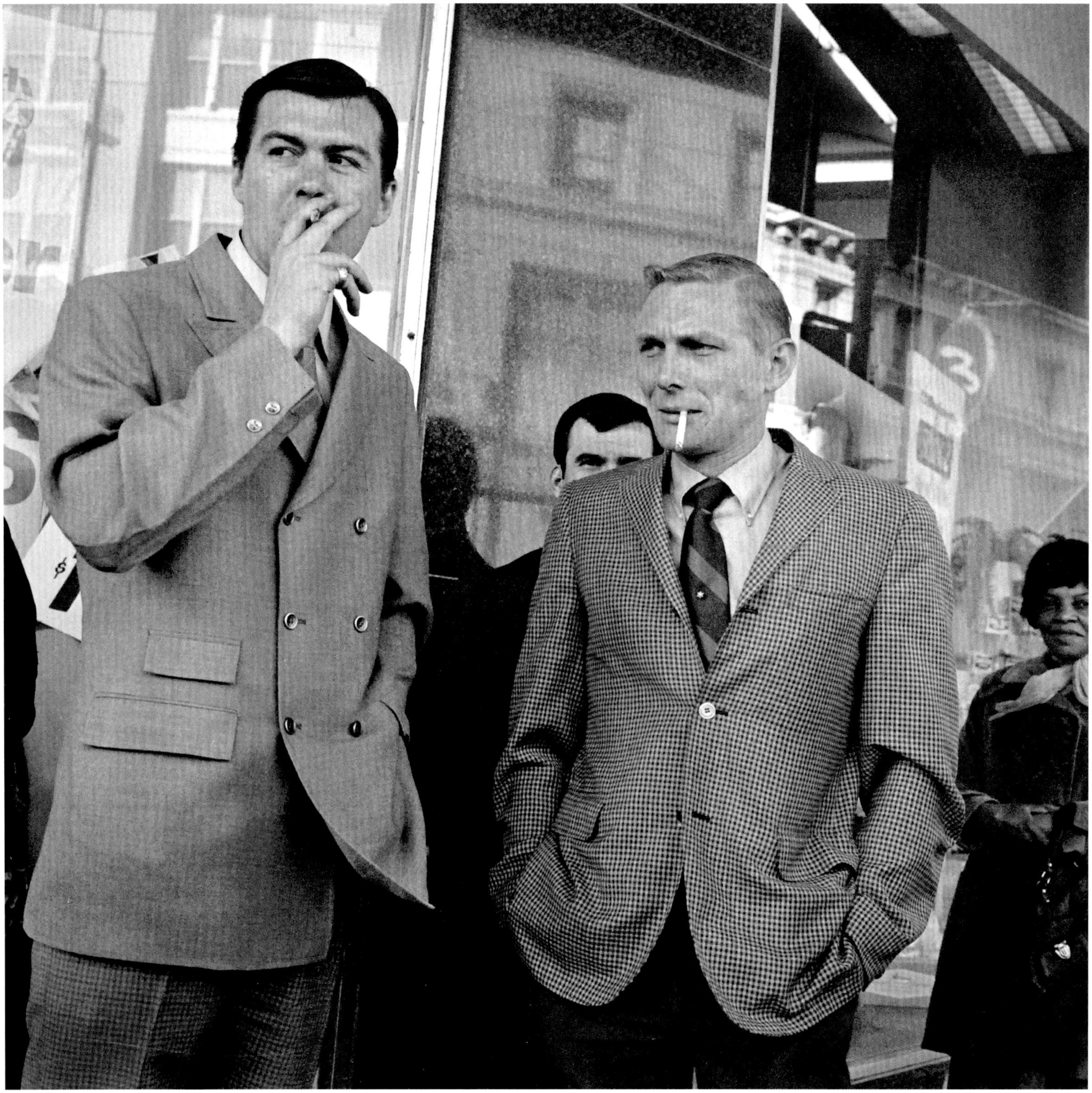

Two Men Smoking, Market Street

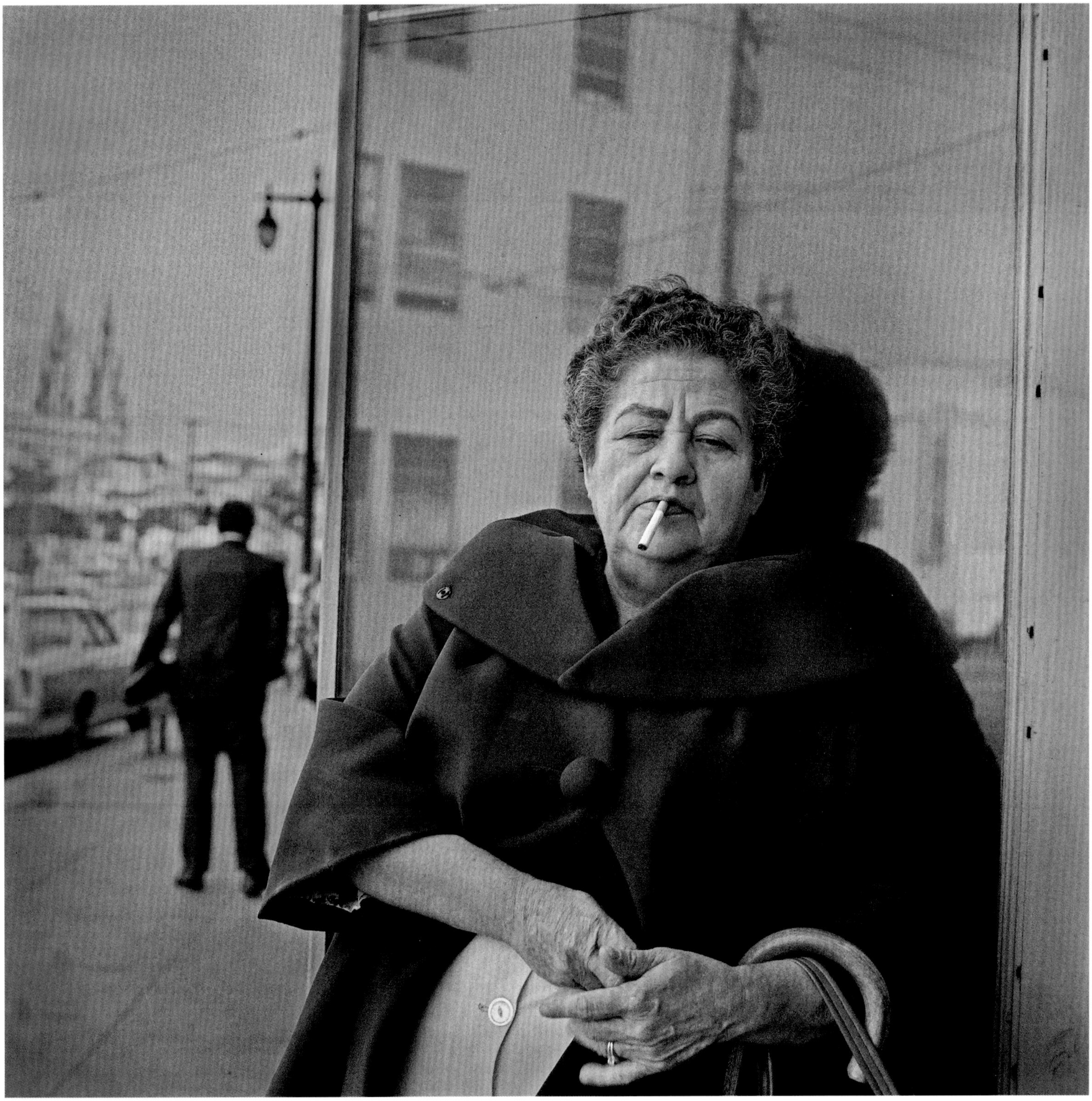

Woman with Cigarette and Man with Briefcase, North Beach

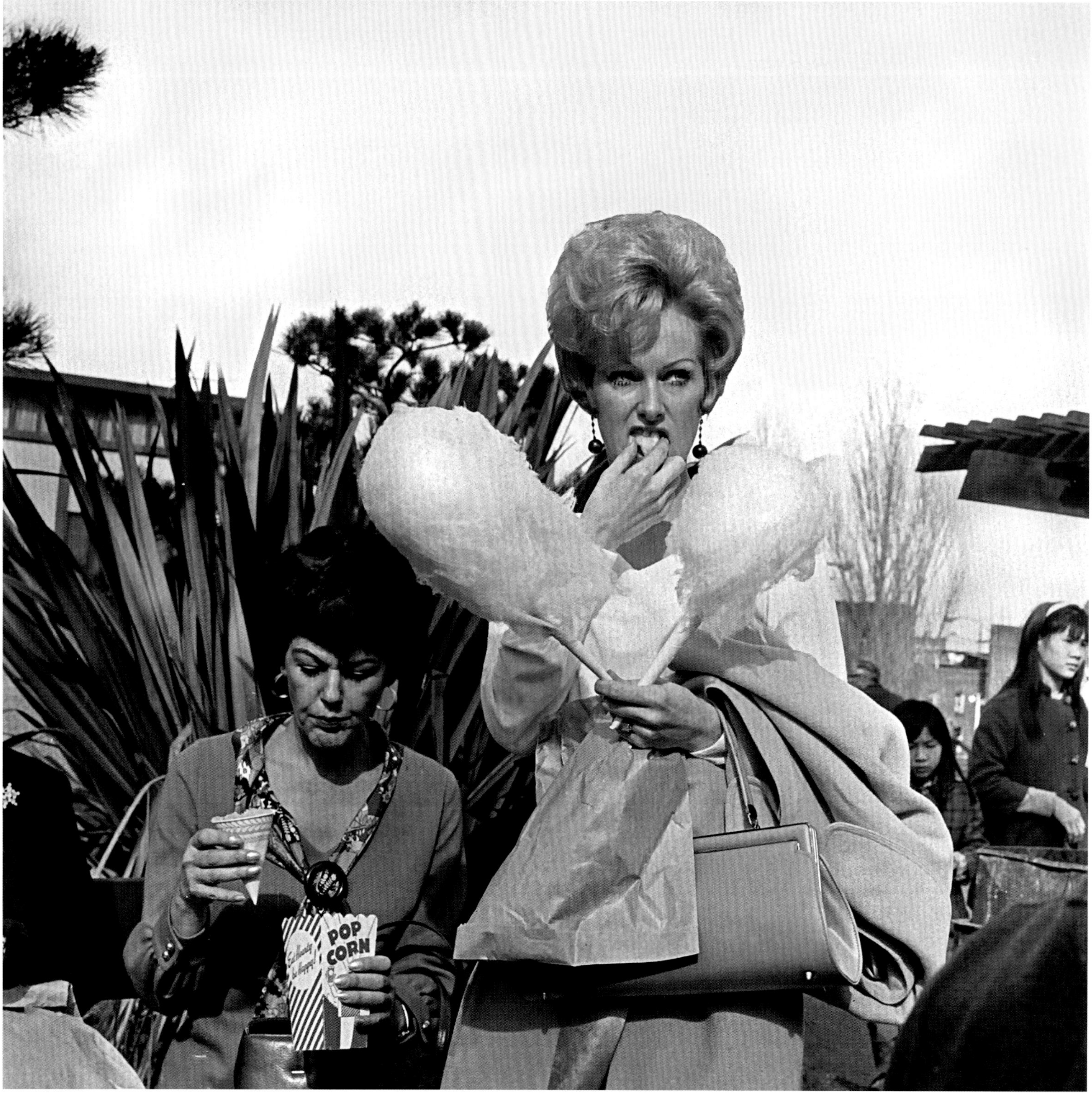

Popcorn and Cotton Candy

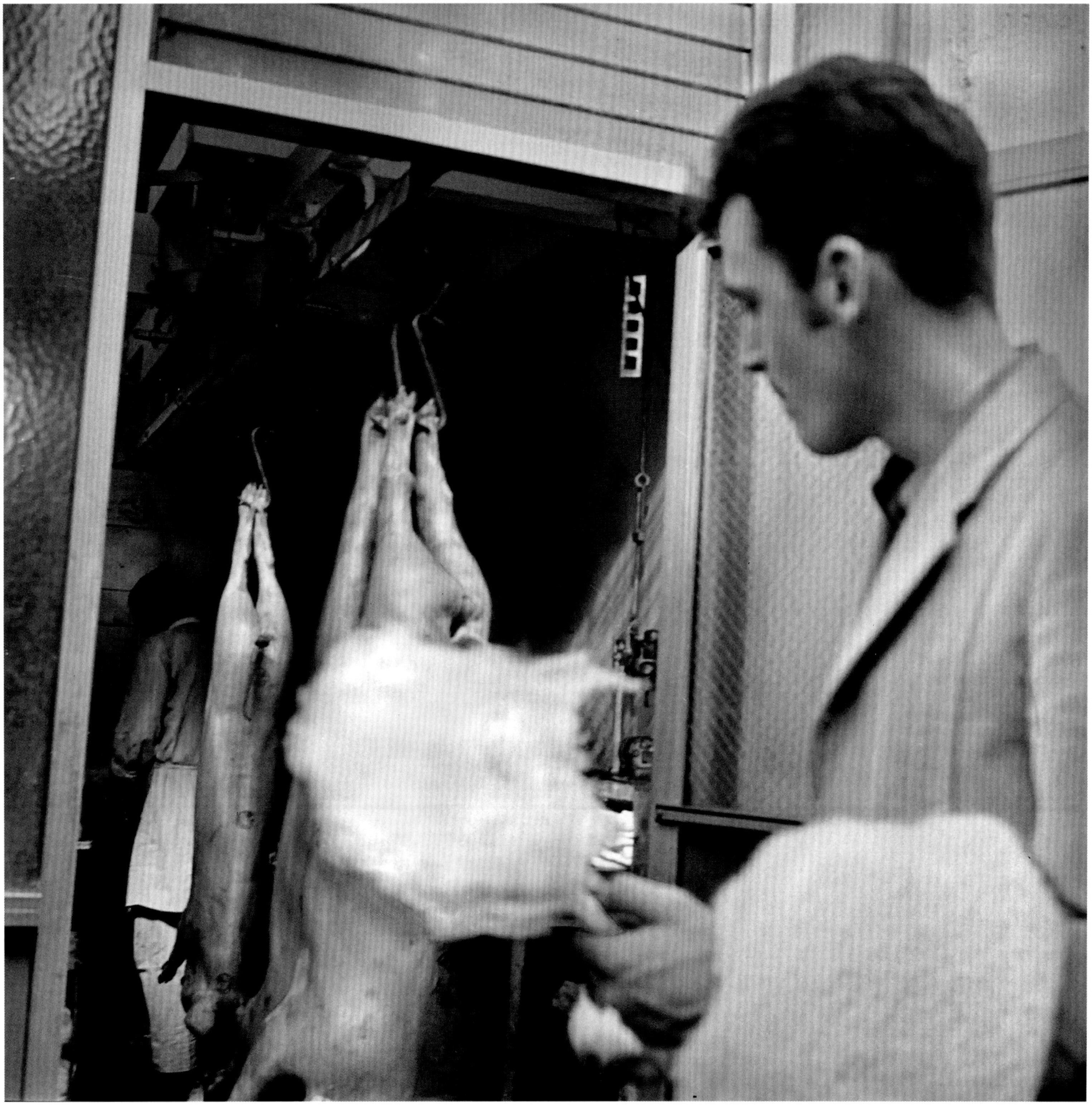

Cotton Candy Outside Butcher Shop, Chinatown

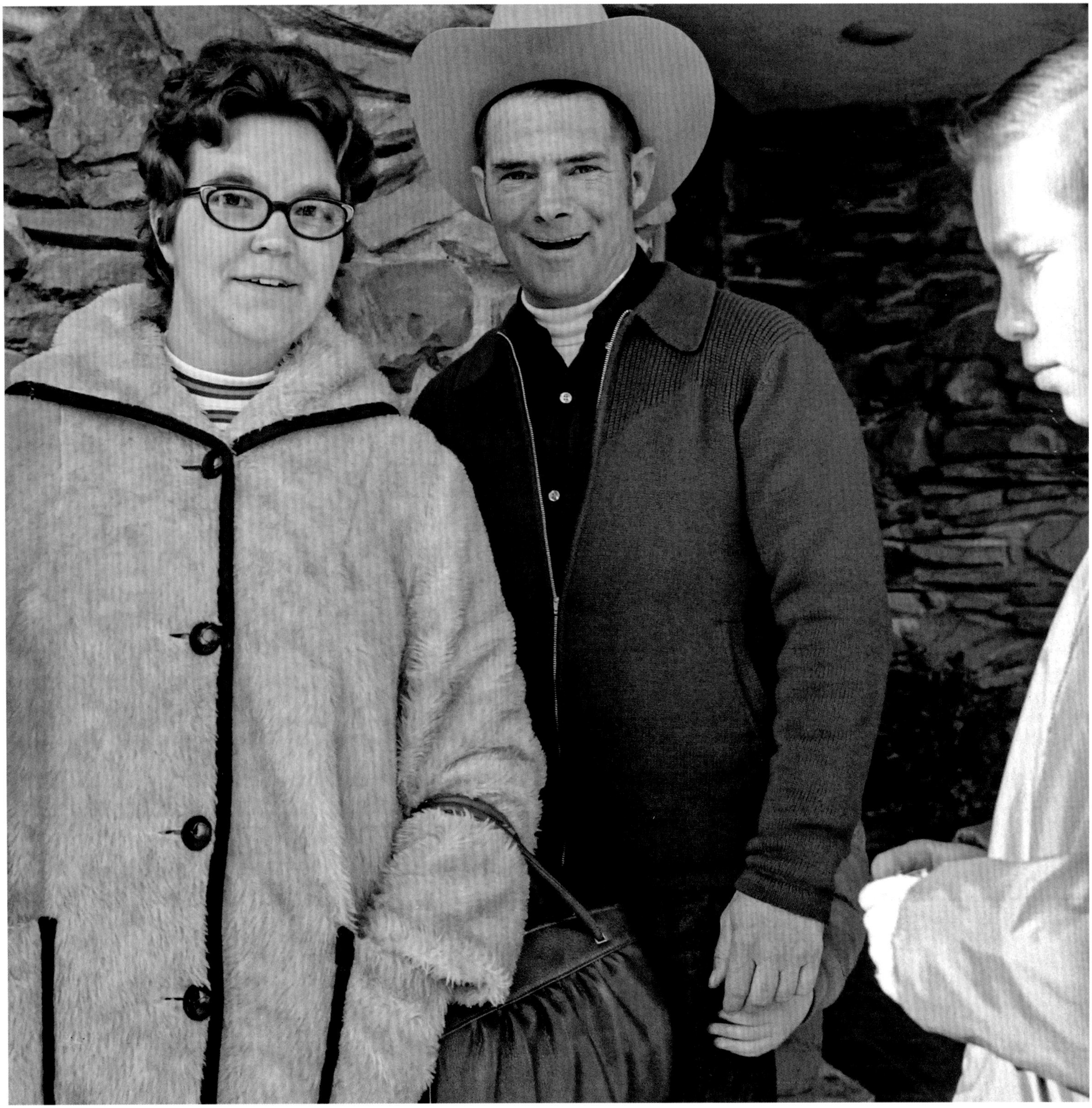

Parents and Son

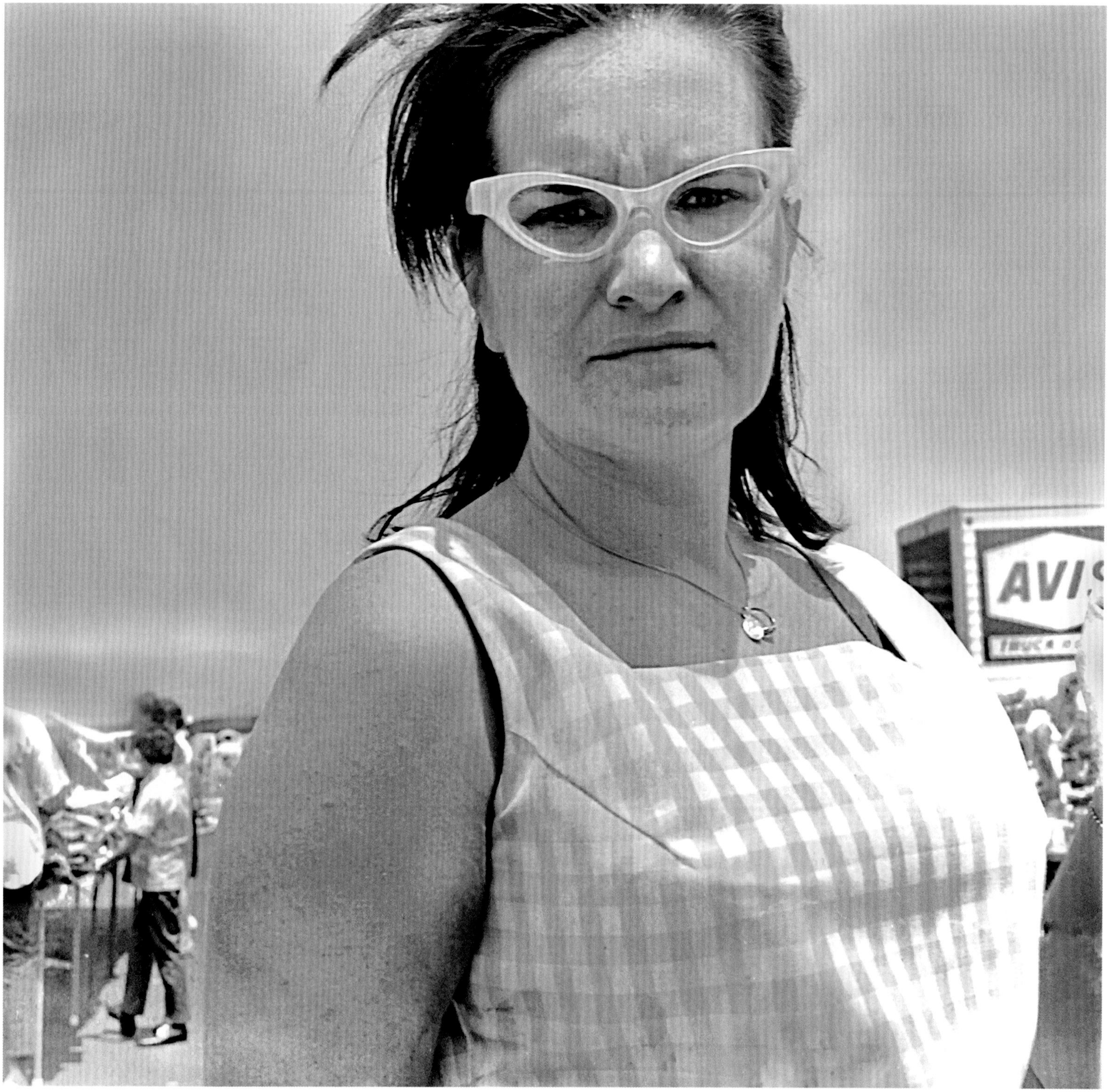

Woman with White-Frame Glasses at Swap Meet, Los Angeles

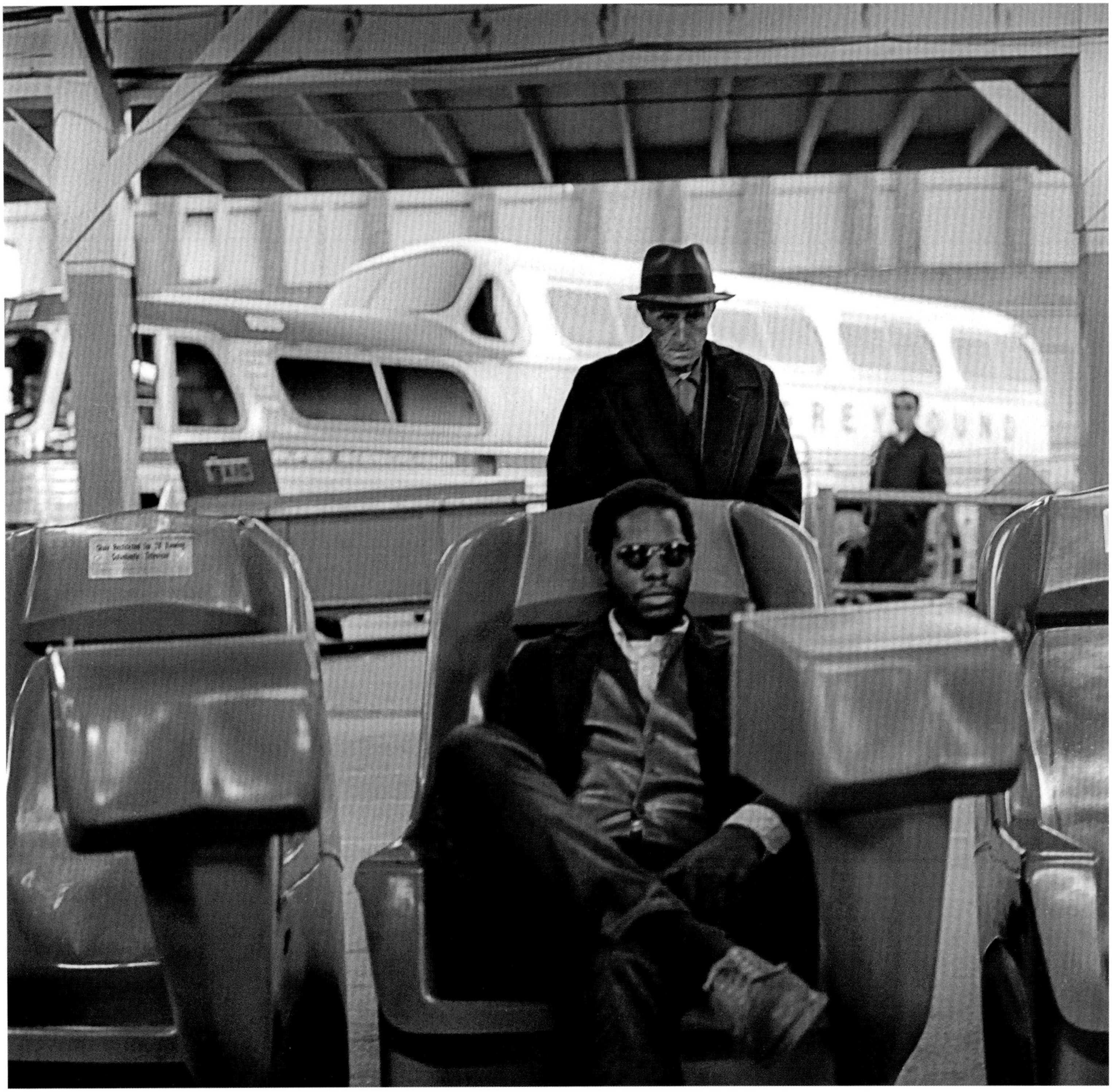

Men Watching TV at the Greyhound Bus Terminal

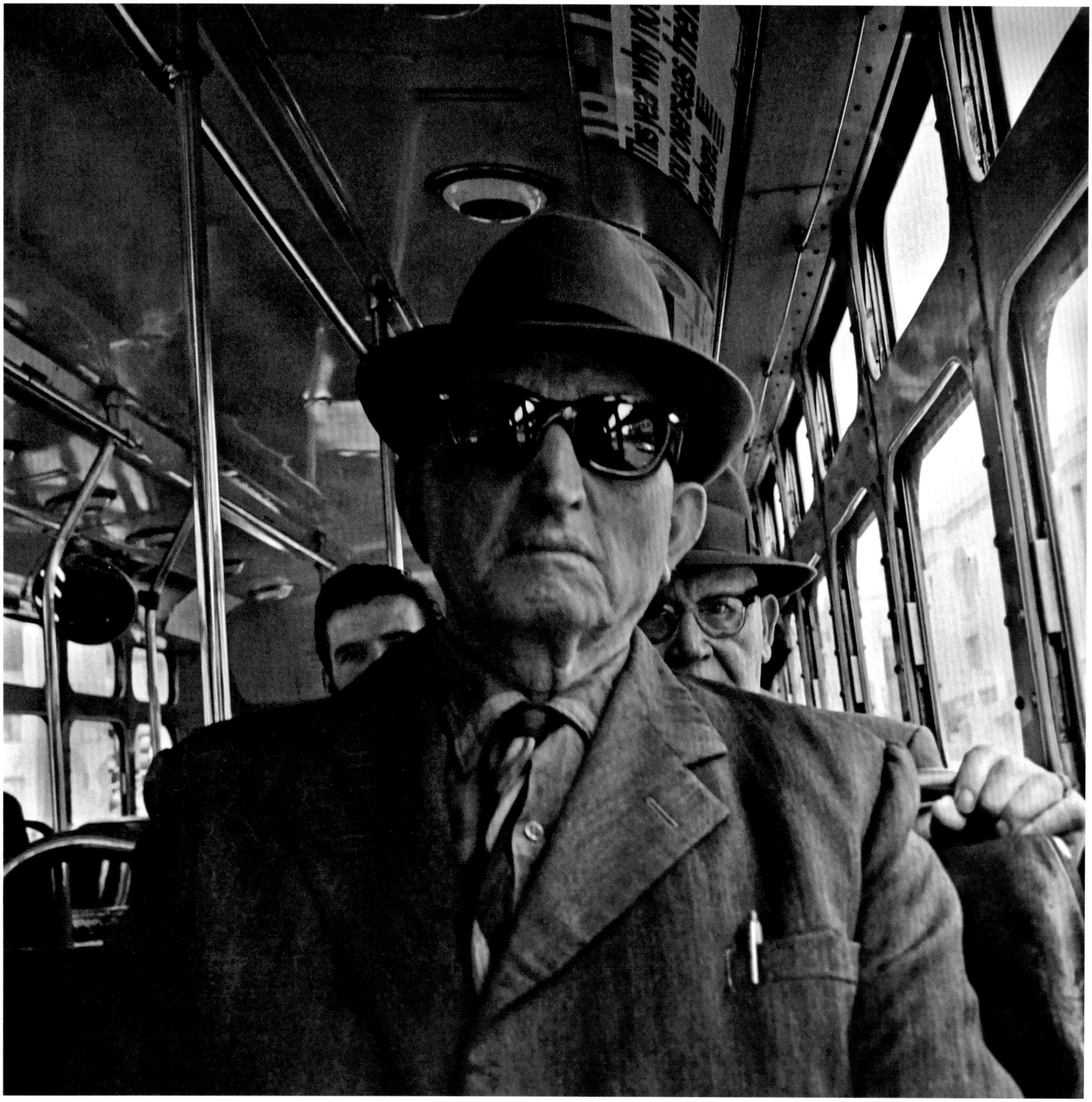

Three Men on MUNI, North Beach

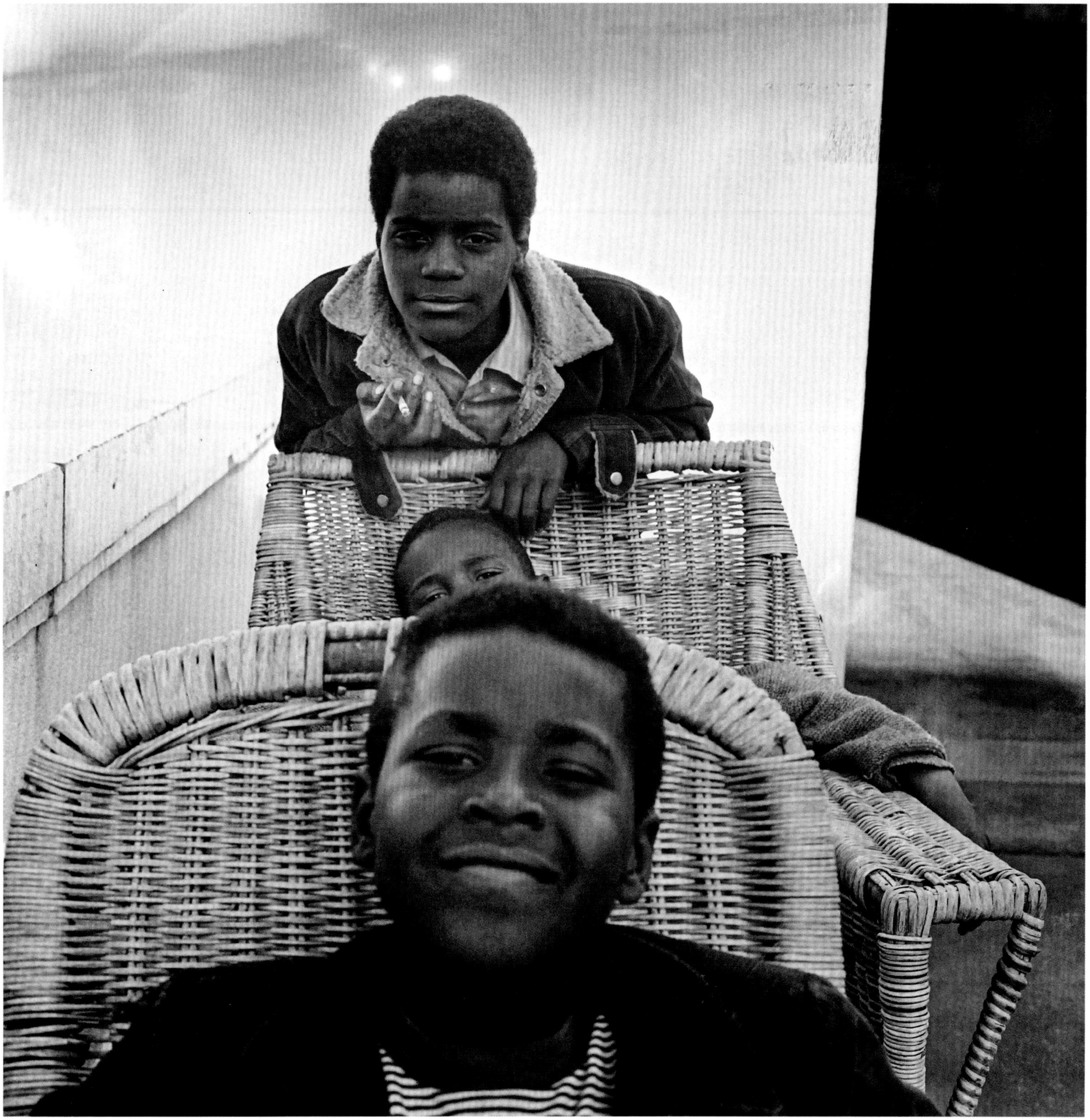

Three Boys in Wicker Chairs

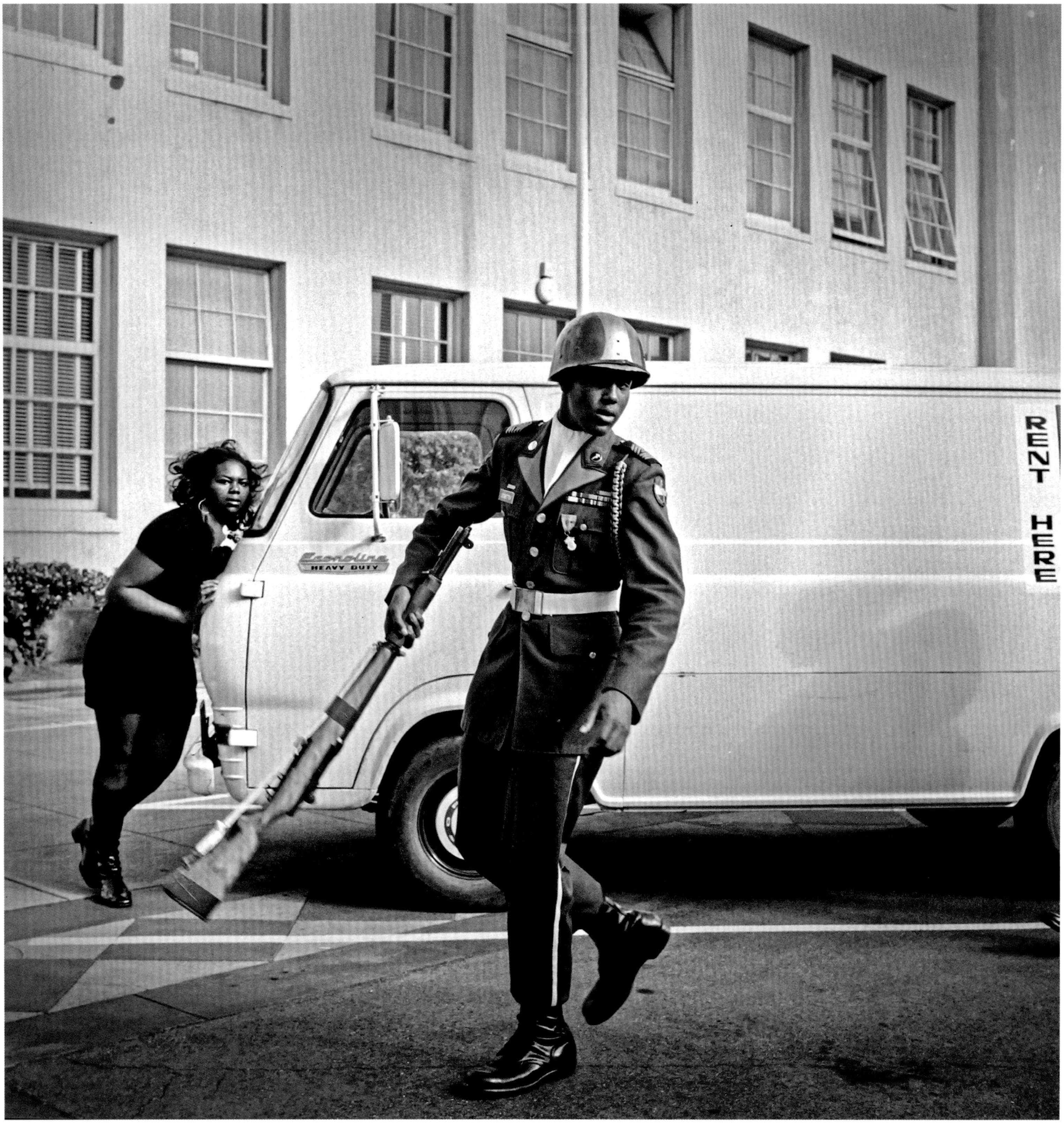

ROTC Couple at Parade Rehearsal

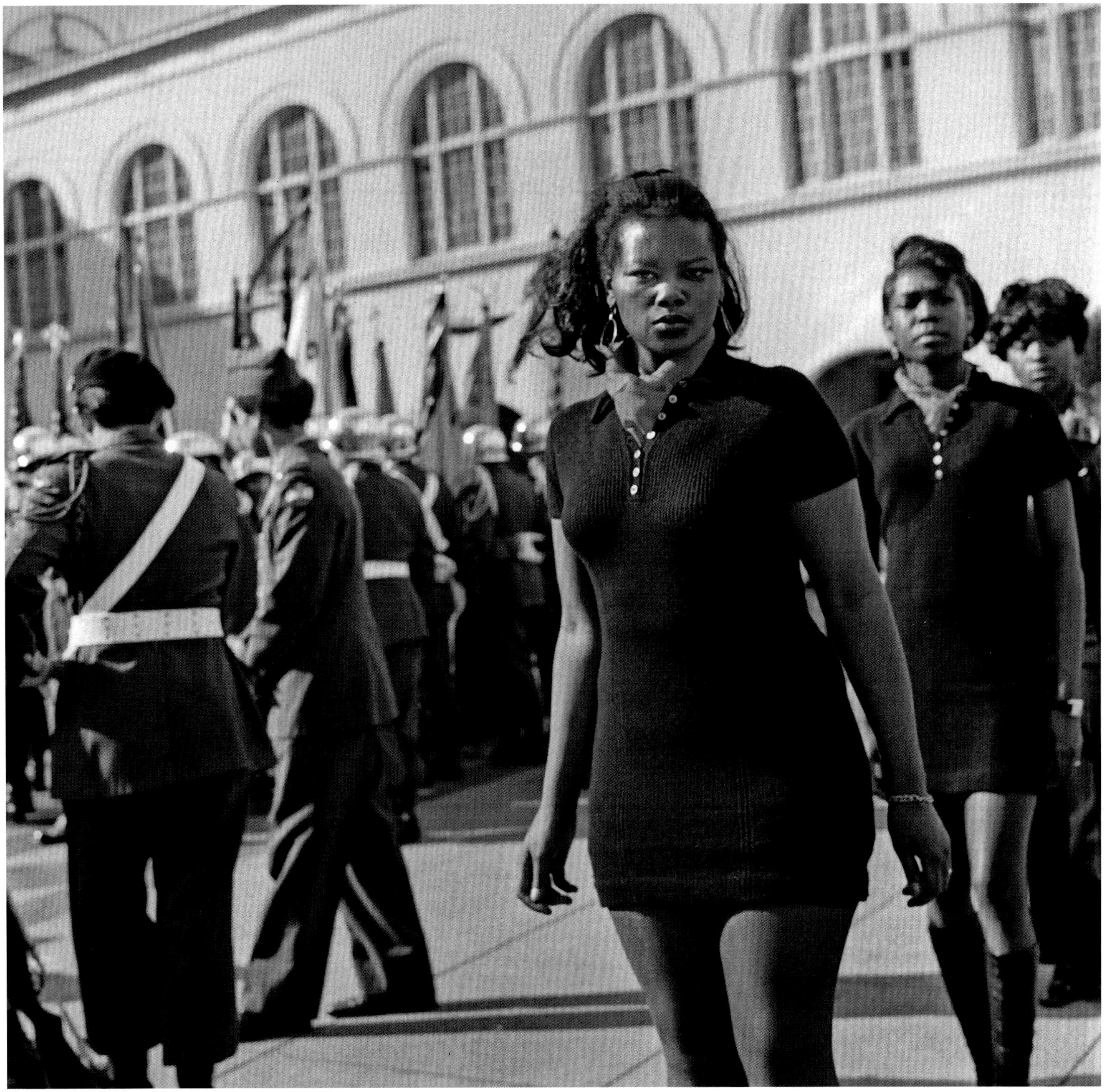

ROTC Drill Team at the Board of Education Building

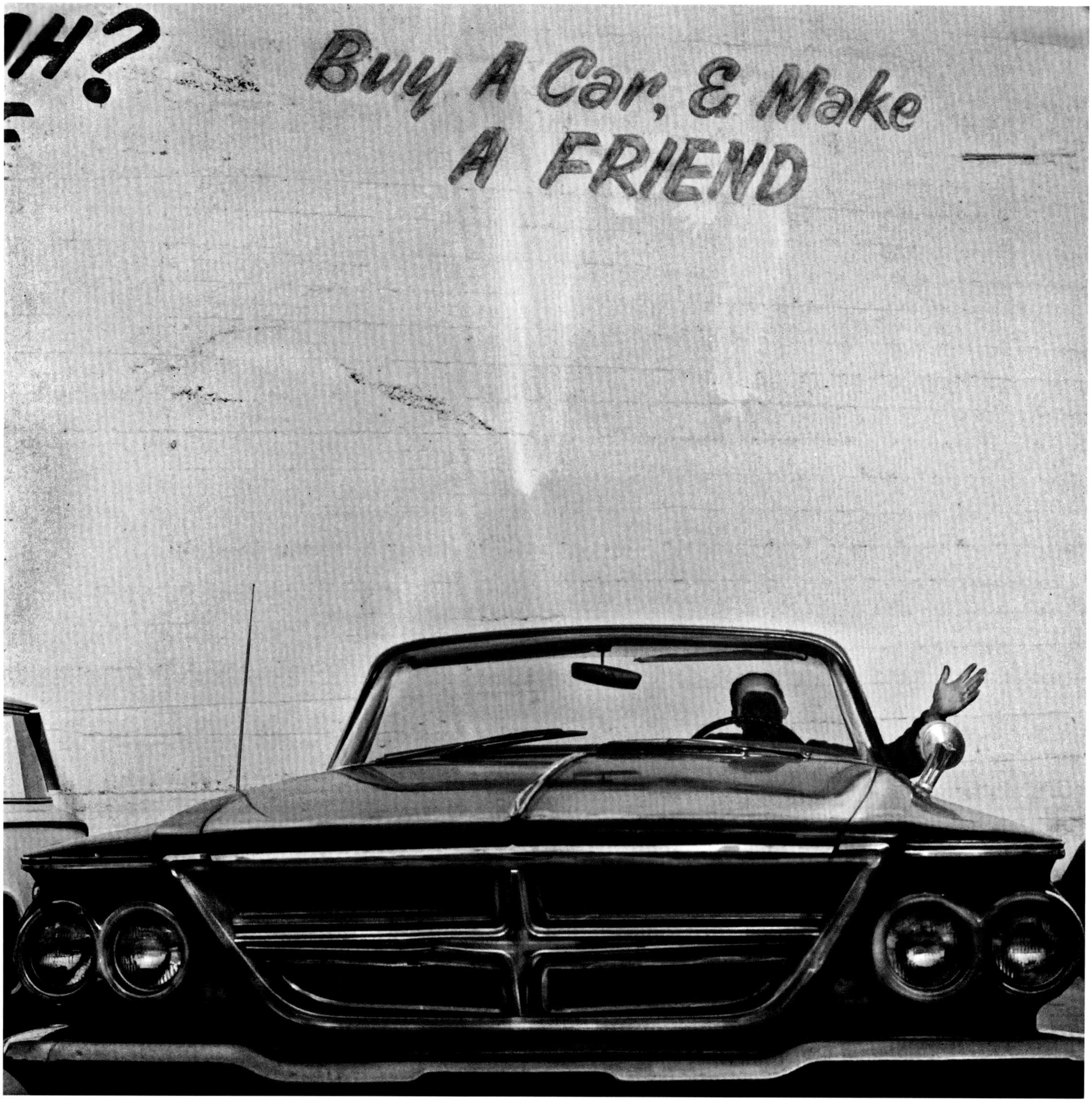

Buy a Car and Make a Friend, Los Angeles

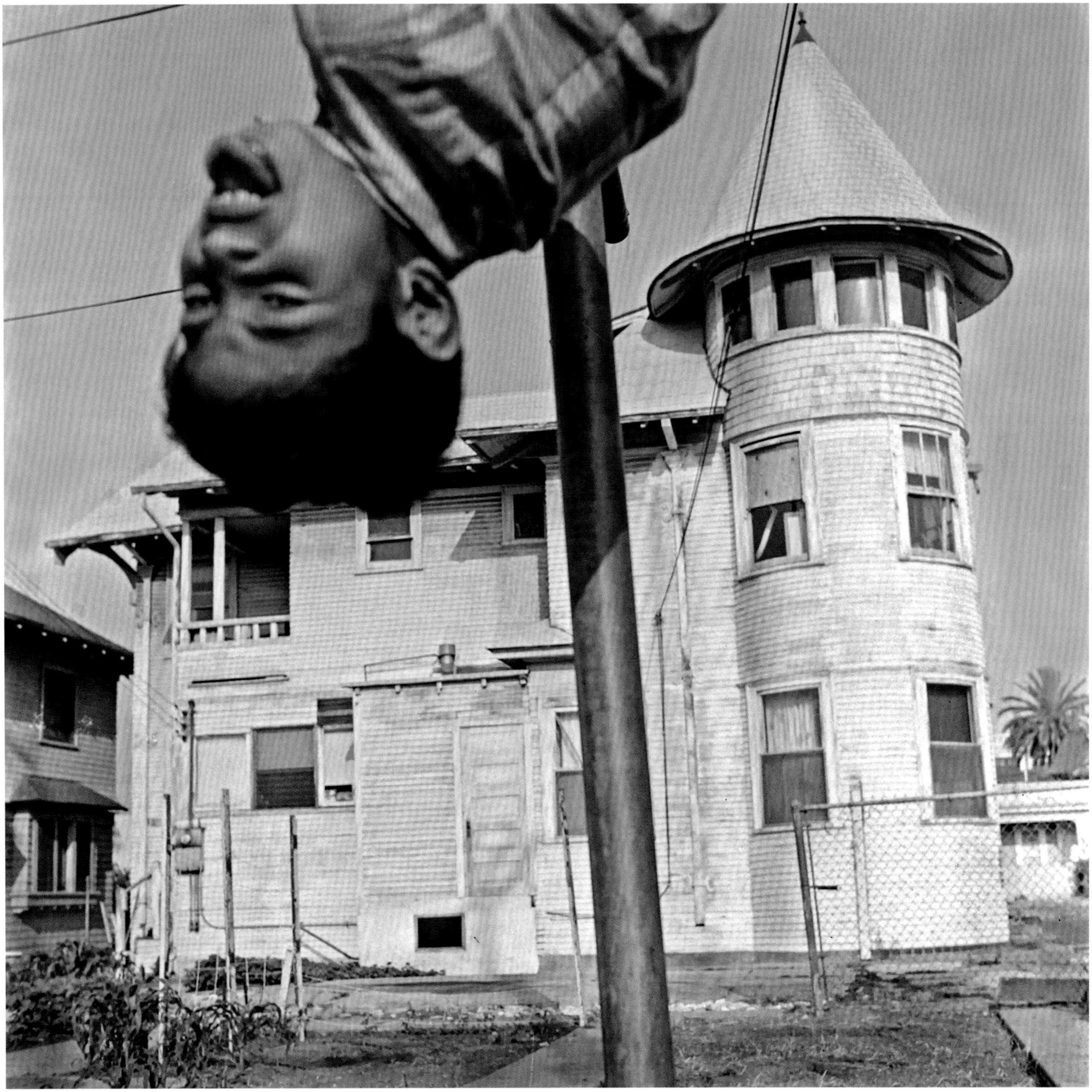

Upside-Down Boy and Witch's Hat, Los Angeles

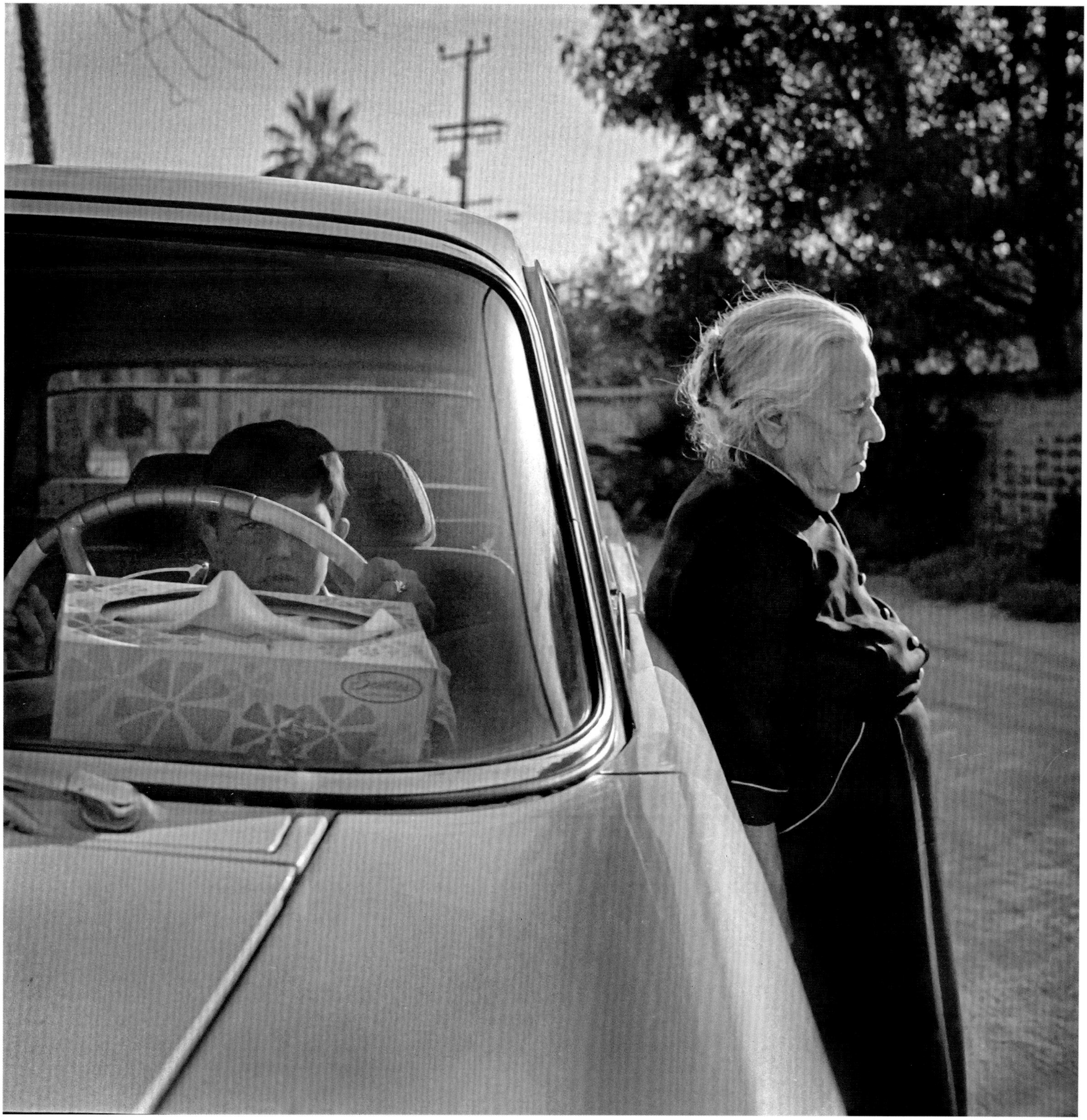

Grandmother and Grandson, Mission San Fernando

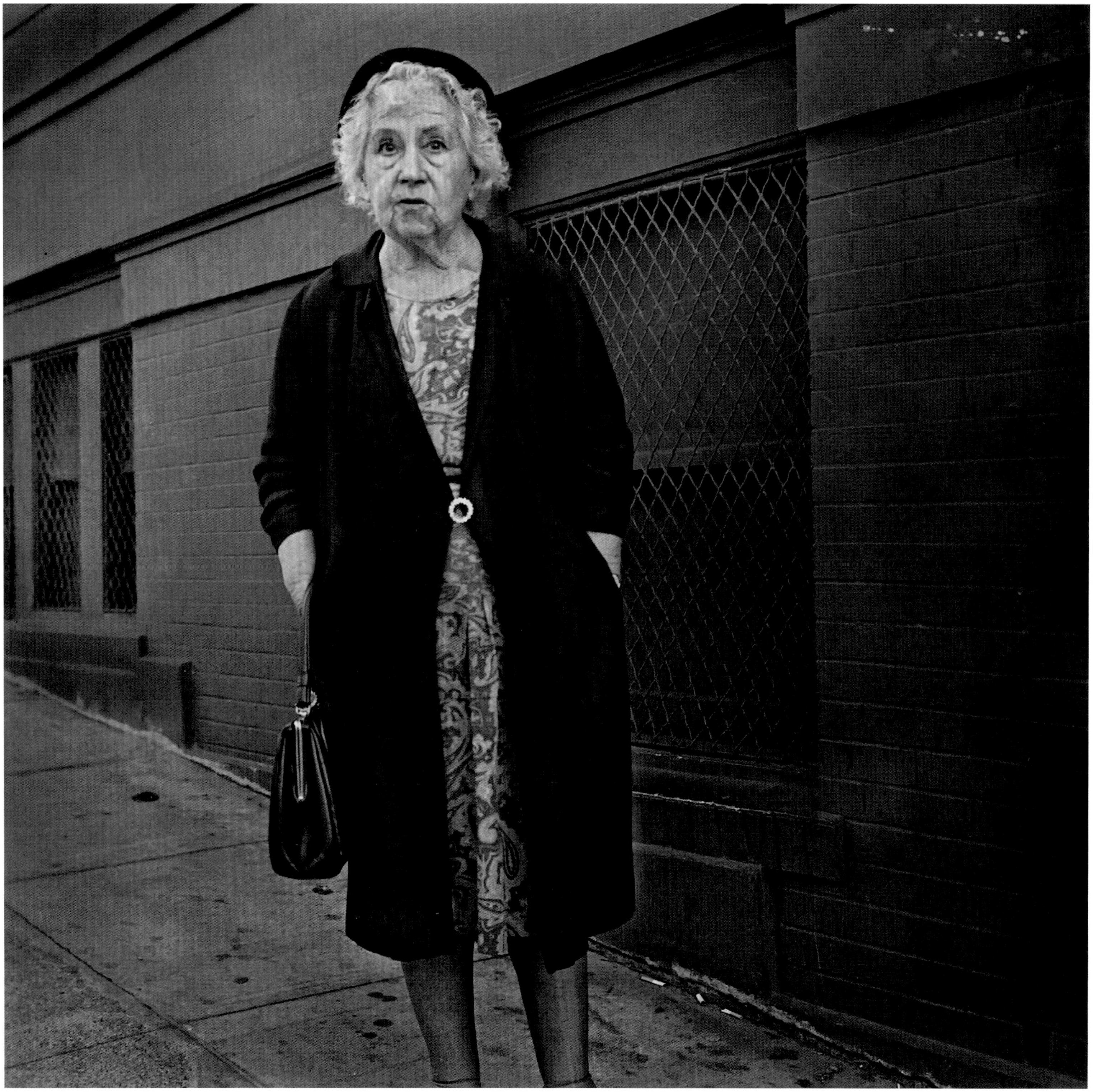

Woman in Black Coat and Paisley Dress, North Beach

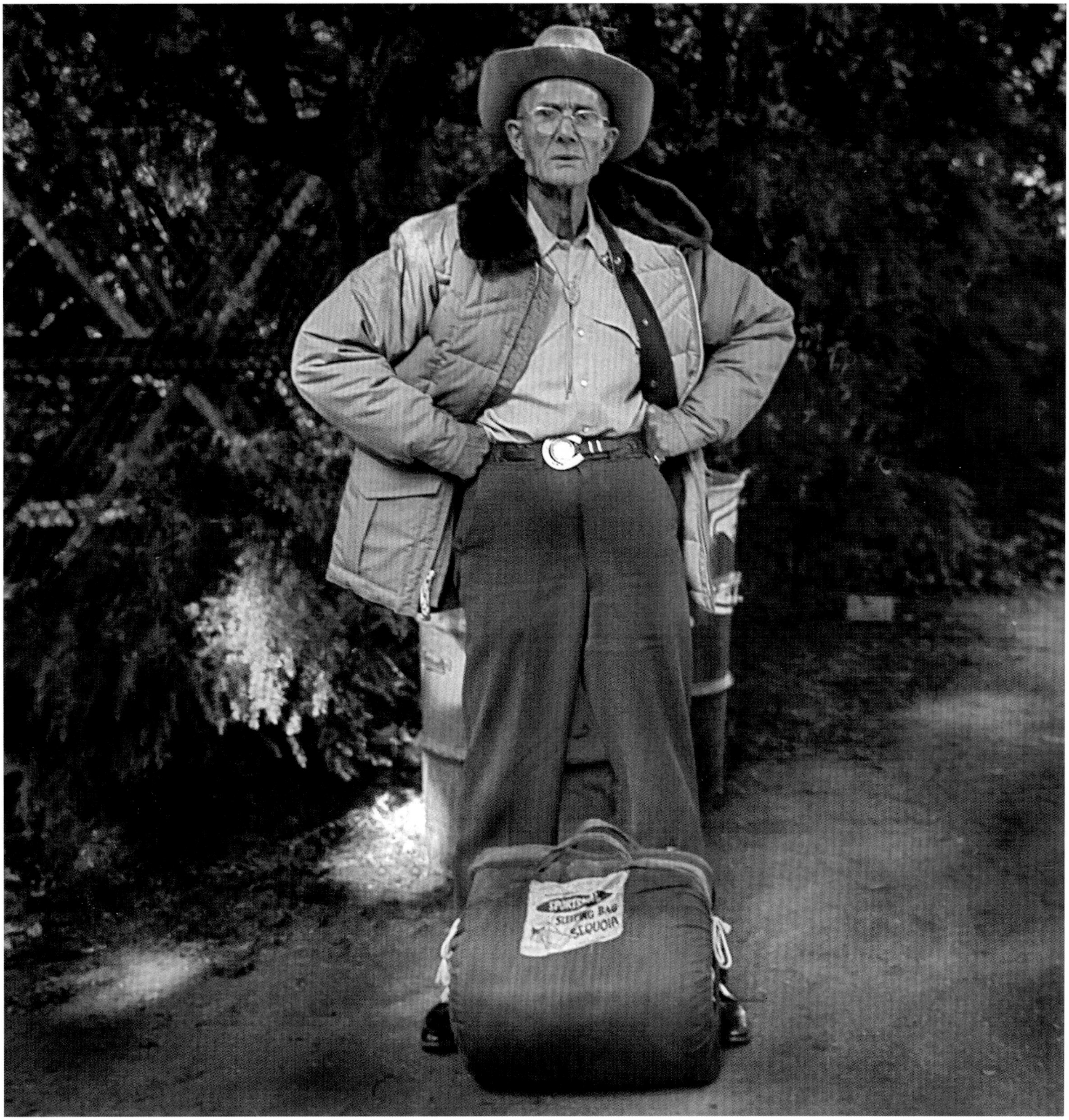

Man with Arms Akimbo, Golden Gate Park

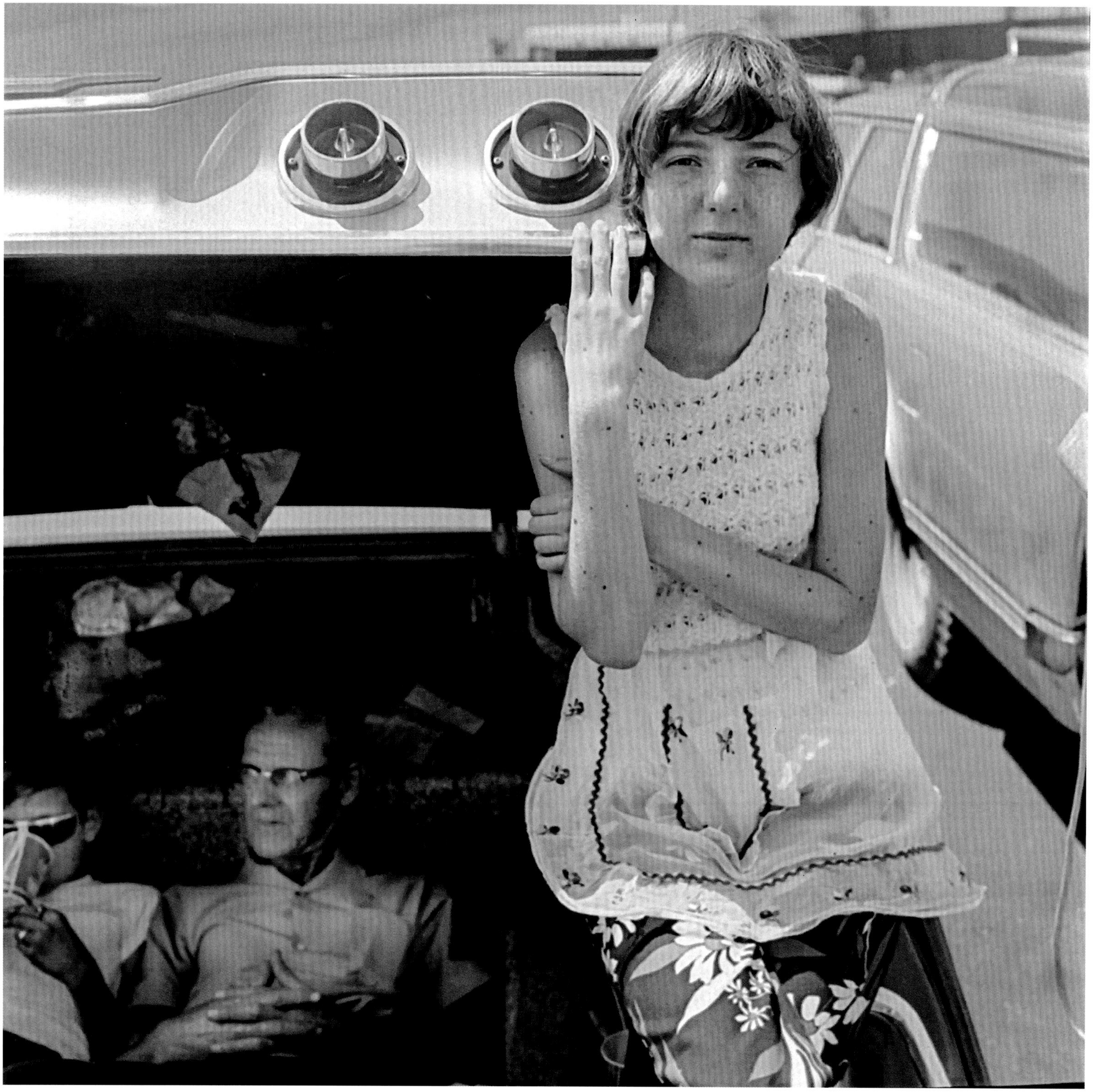

Girl at Swap Meet with Her Father and Brother in the Trunk, Los Angeles

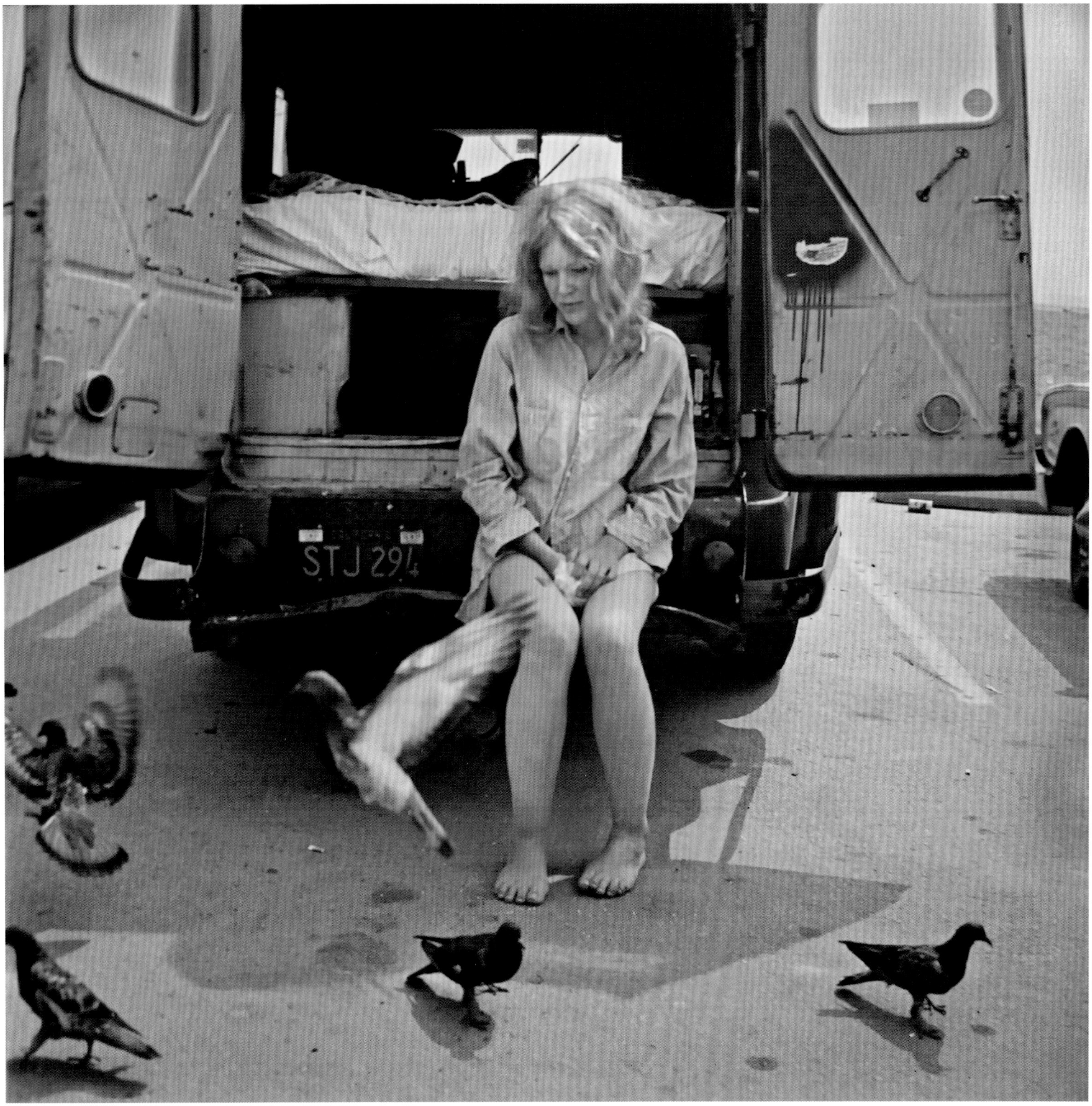

Woman with Pigeons at the Beach, Los Angeles

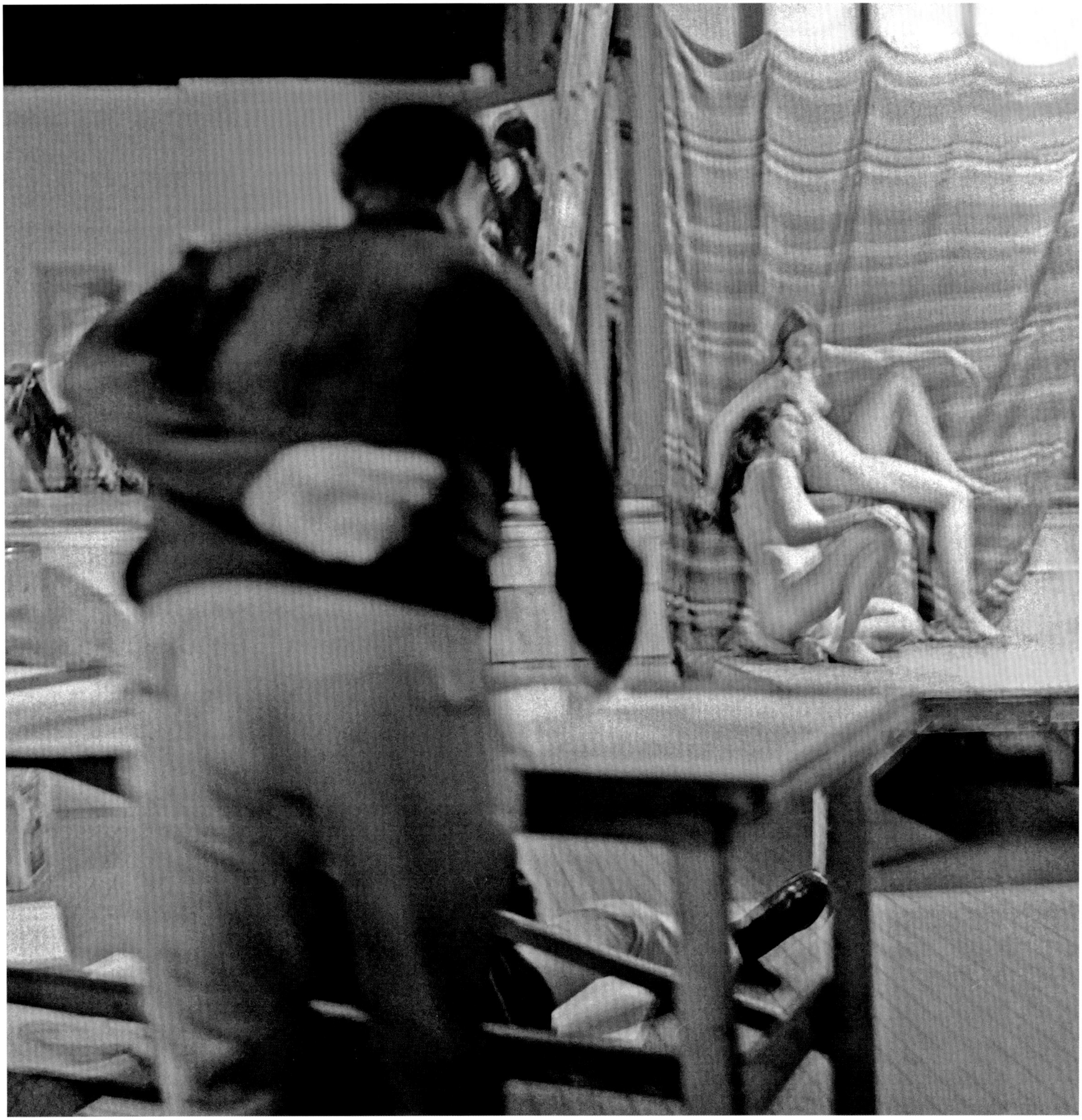

Drawing Class, San Francisco Art Institute

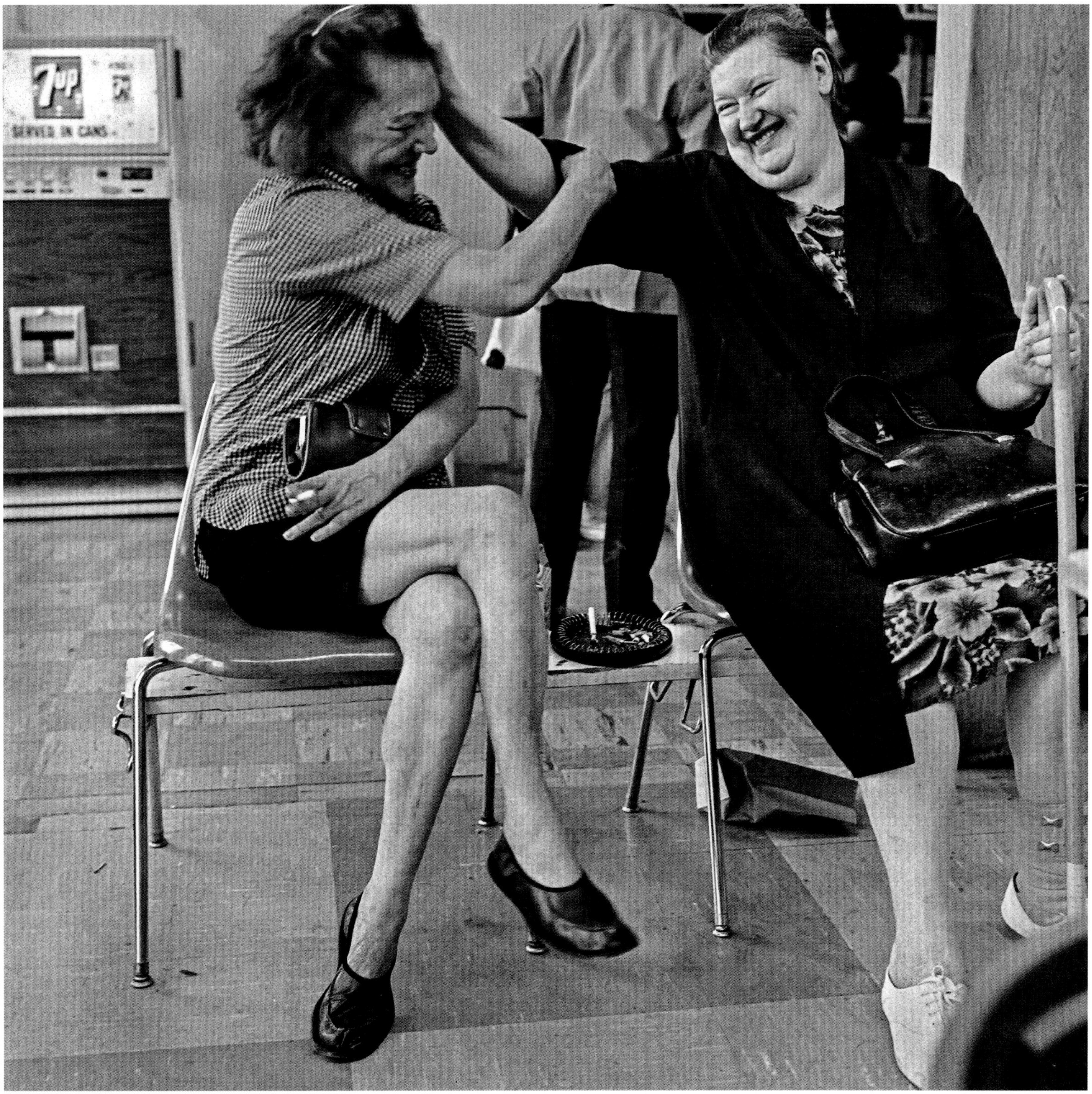

Friends in Laundromat, Leavenworth Street

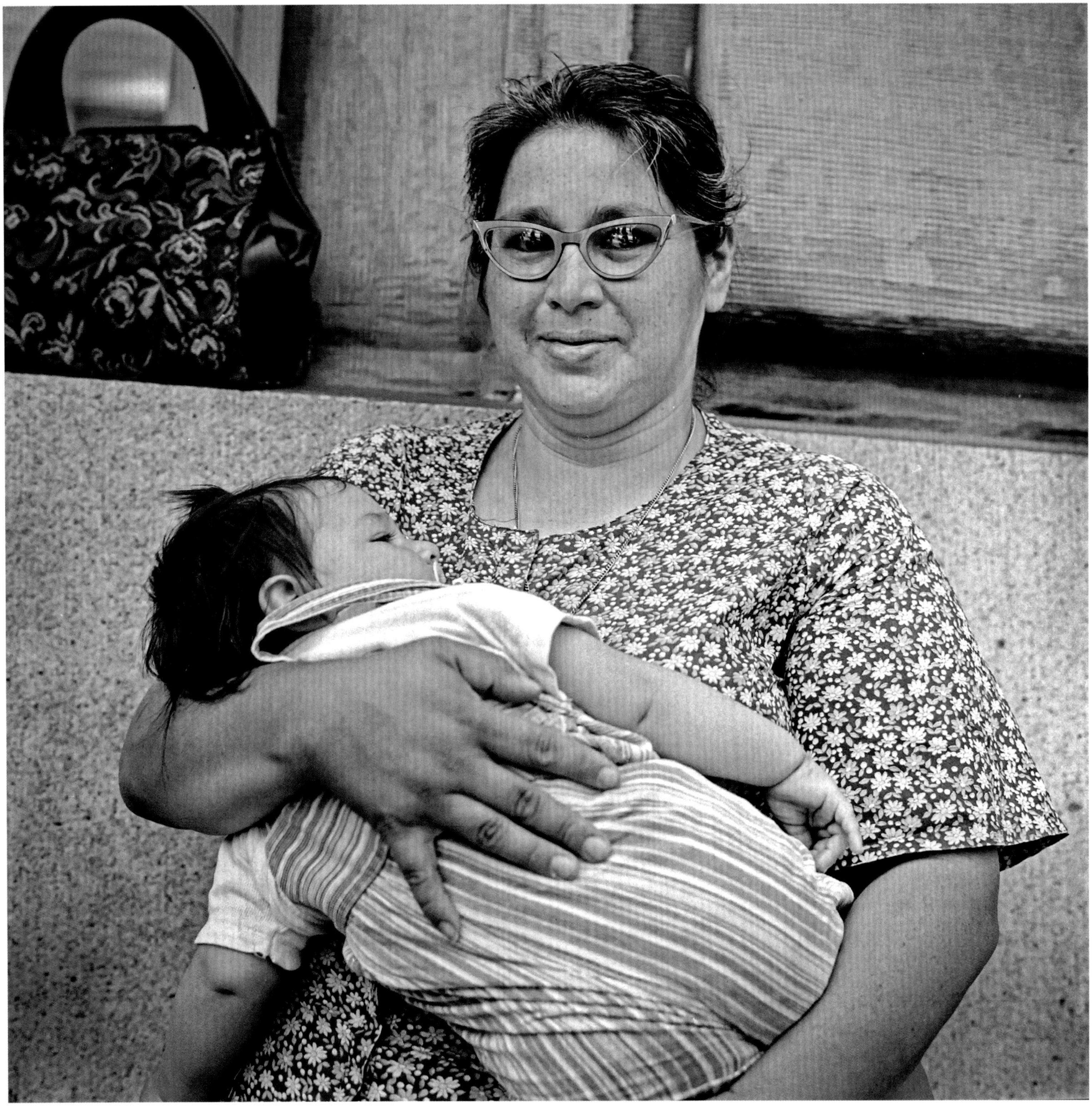

Woman Holding Child

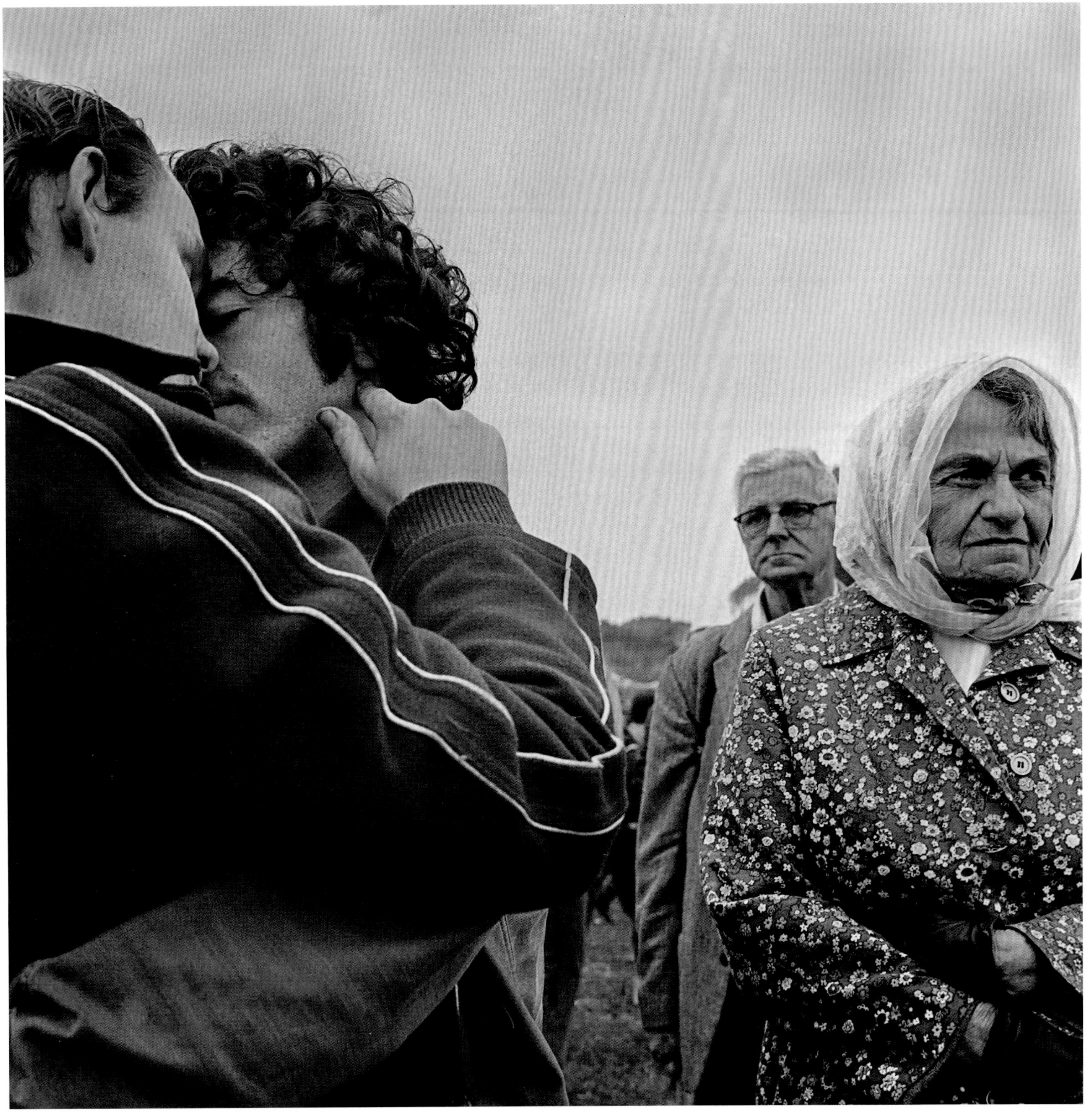

Men Kissing at Peace Rally, Golden Gate Park

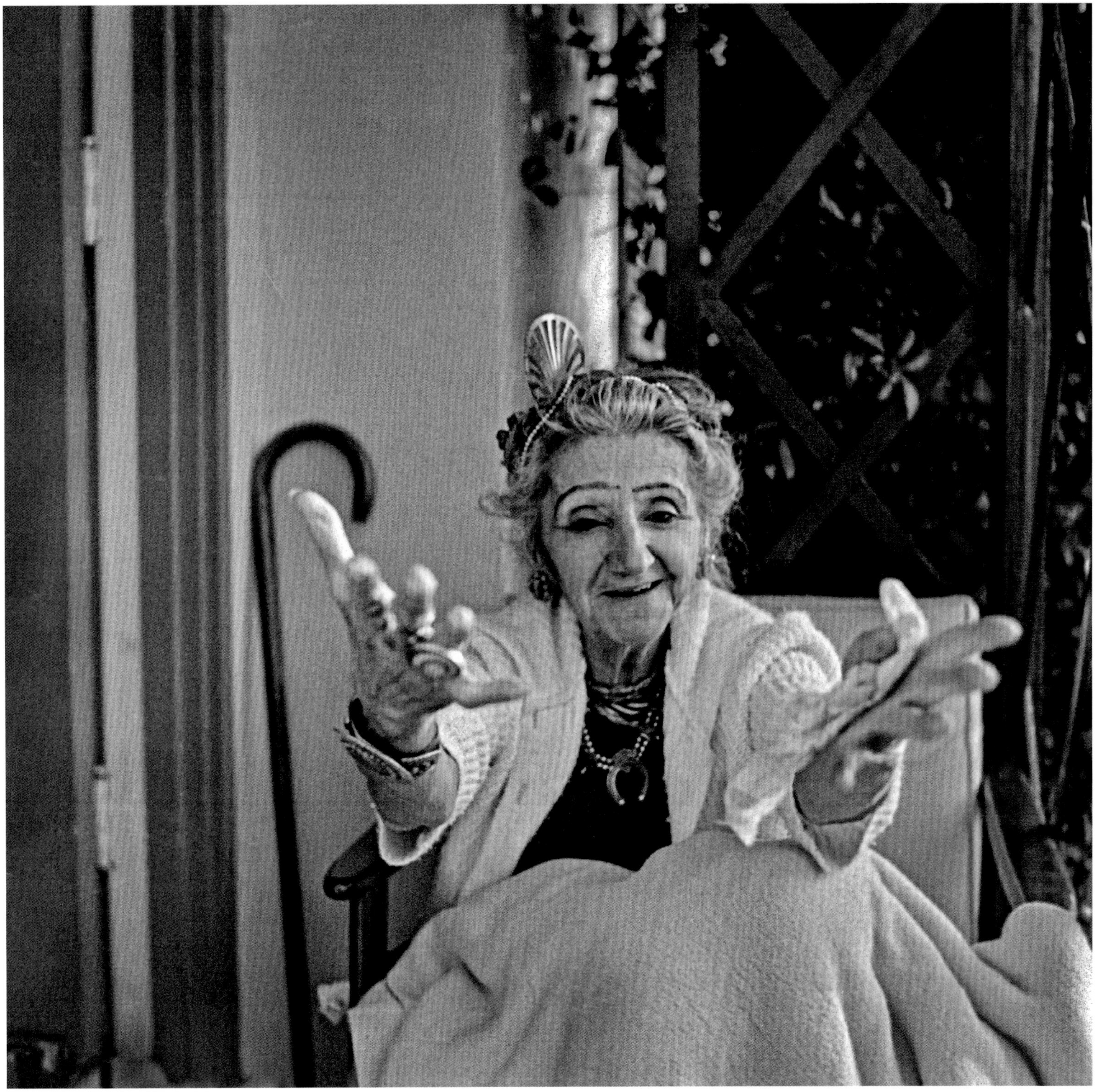

Bejeweled Woman Reaching Out, Venice, California

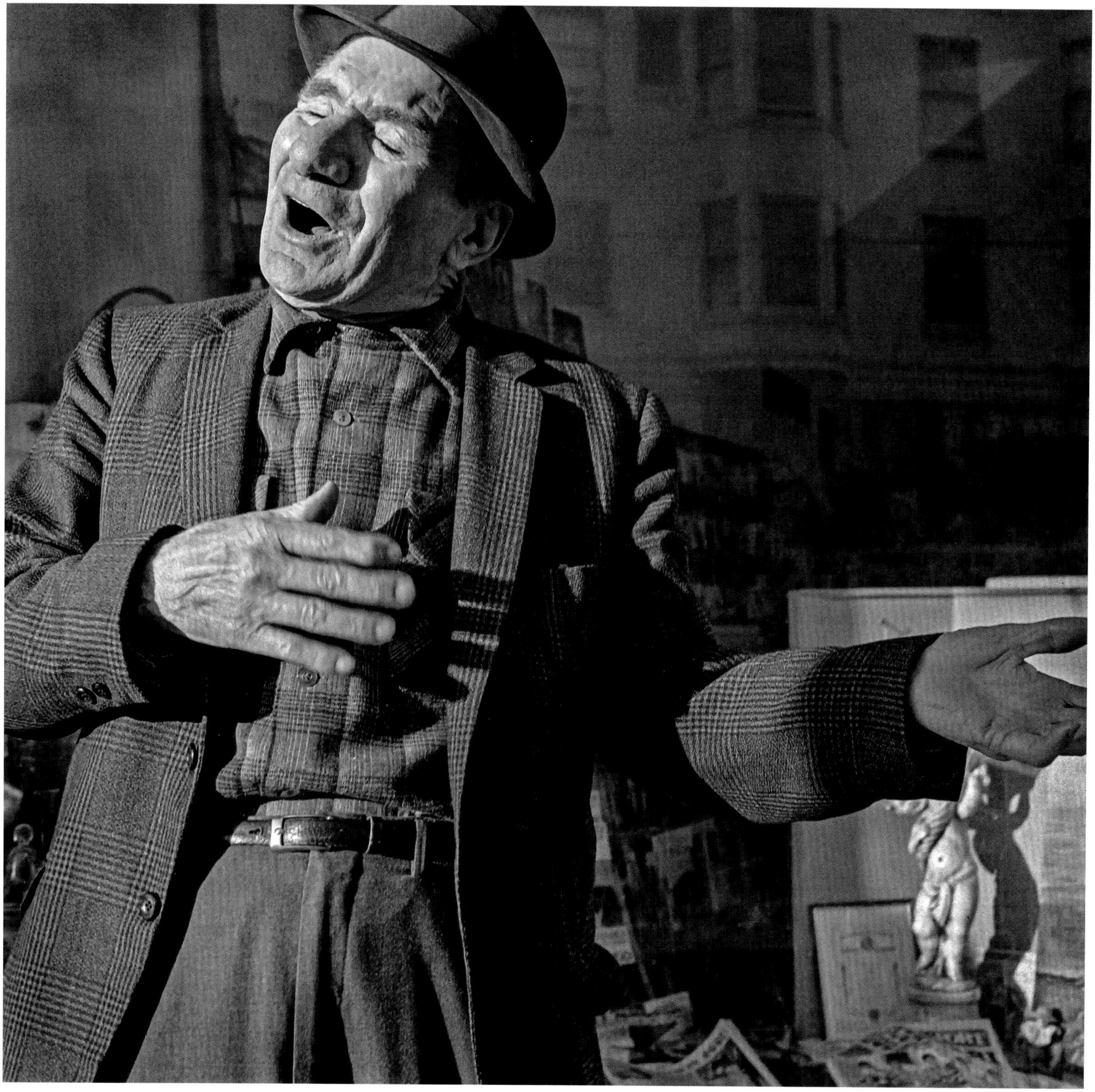

Man Singing, North Beach

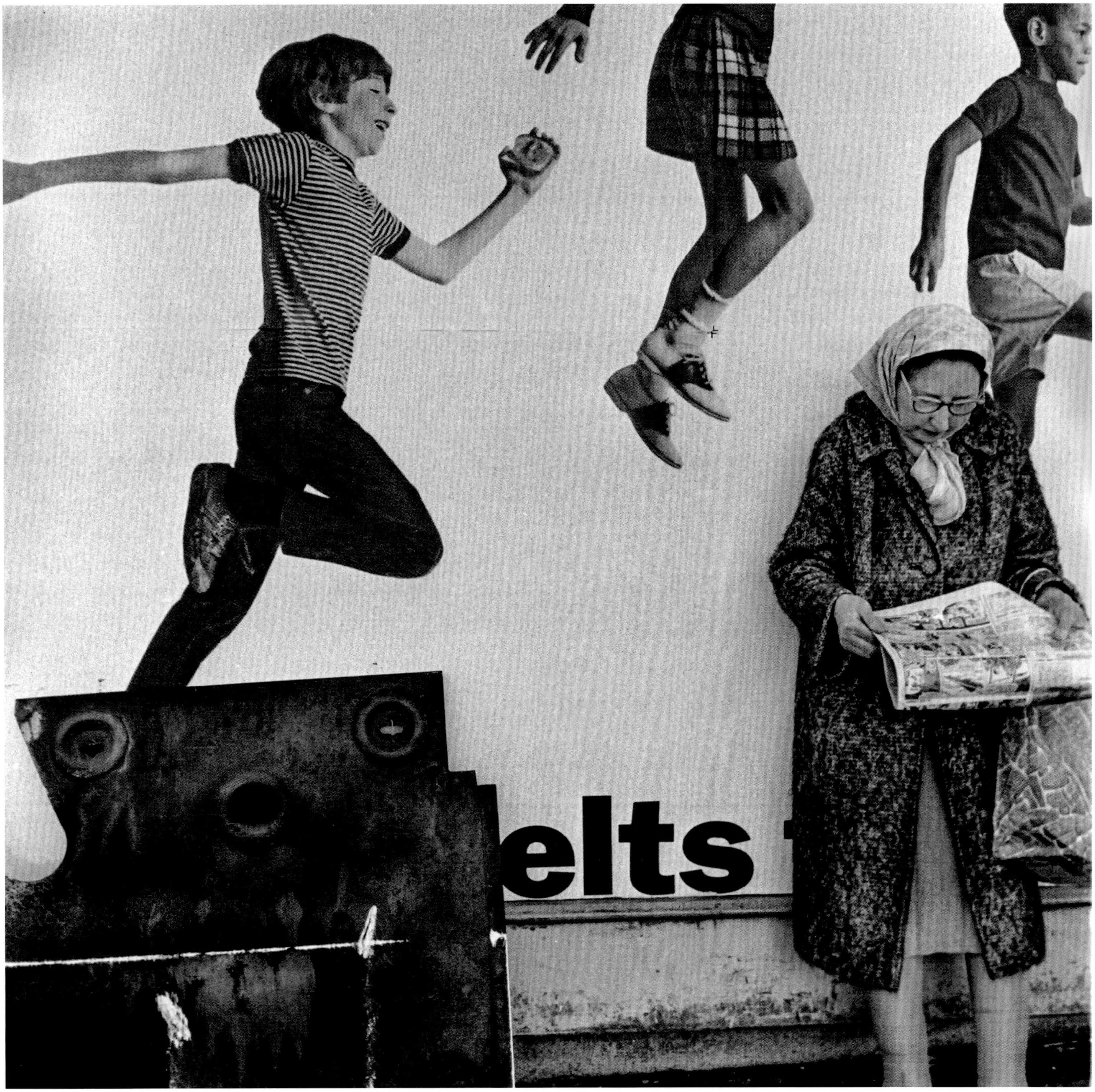

Woman Reading Comics Against Billboard, Downtown

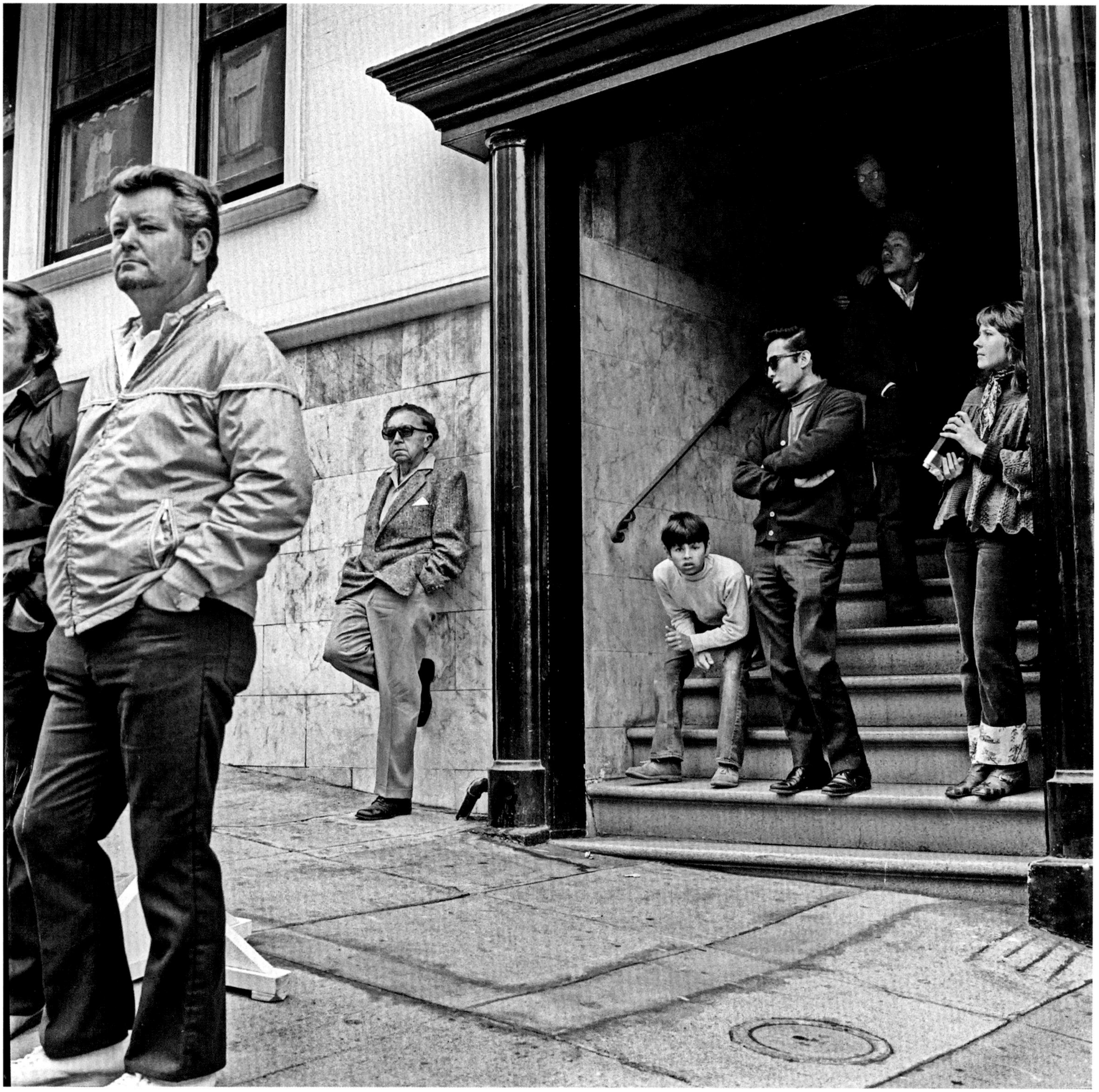

Bus Stop on Leavenworth Street

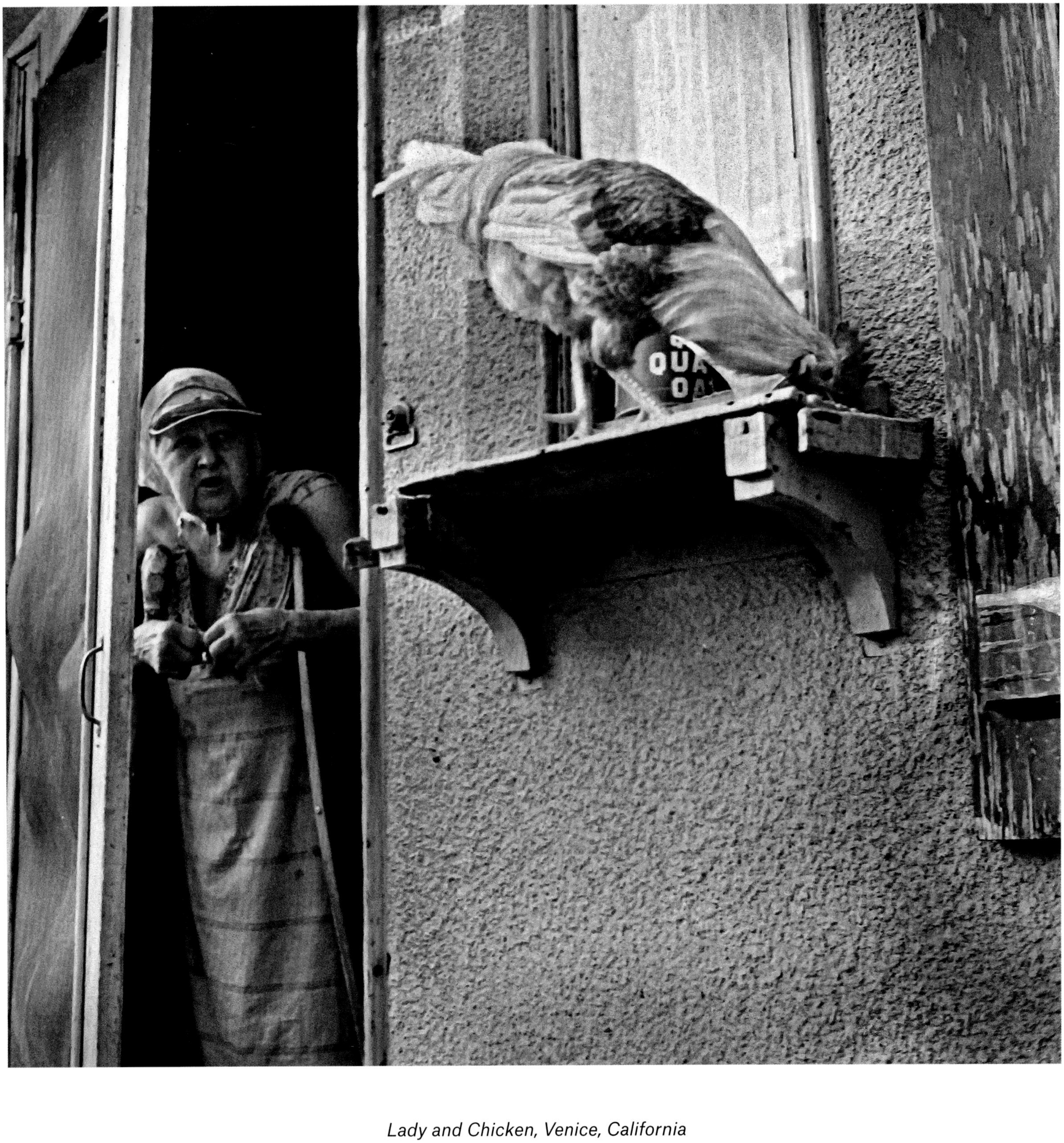

Lady and Chicken, Venice, California

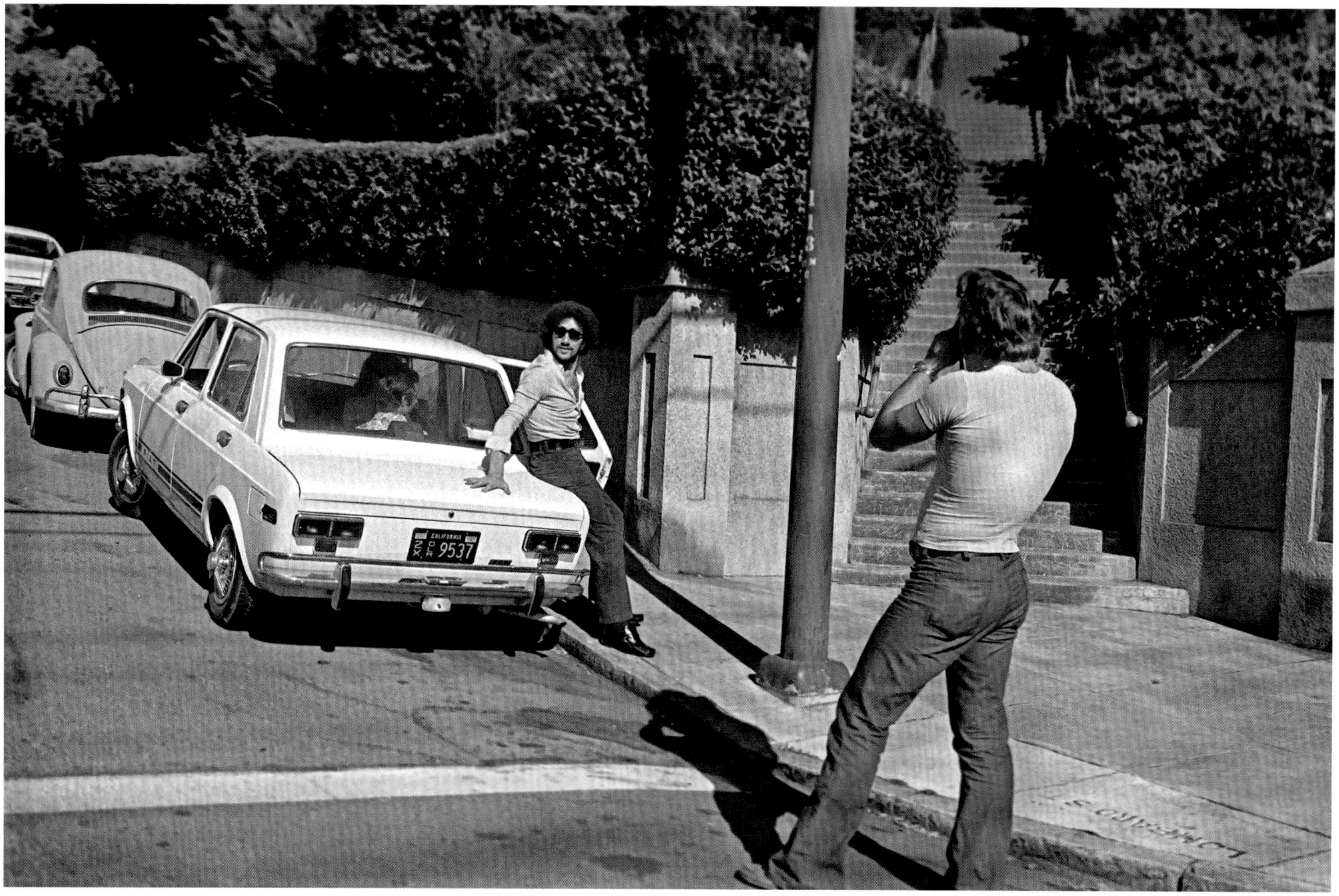

Man Photographing Man, Lombard Street

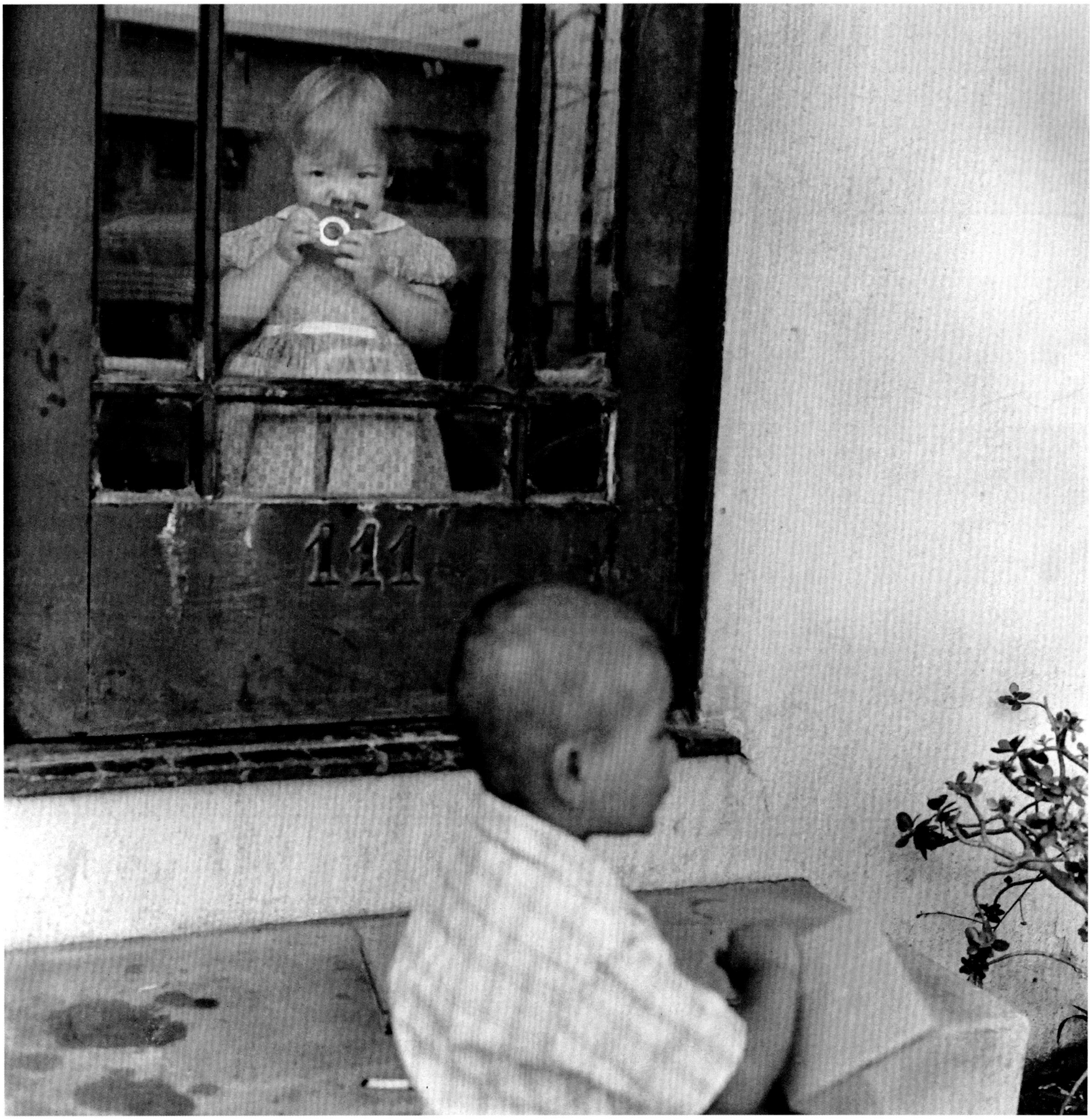

Girl with Camera, San Fernando Valley

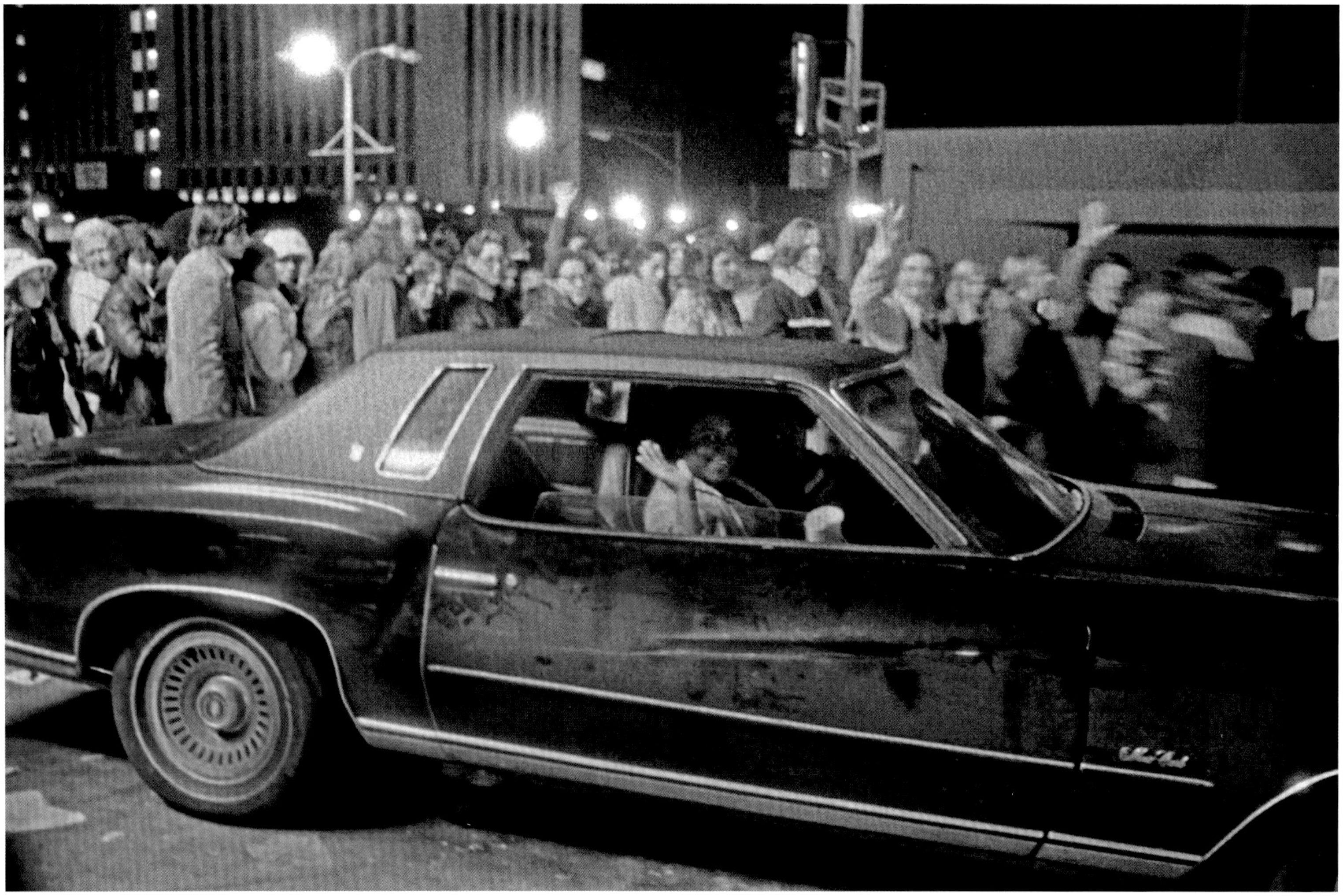

Waiting for The Exorcist, *Moviegoers in Los Angeles*

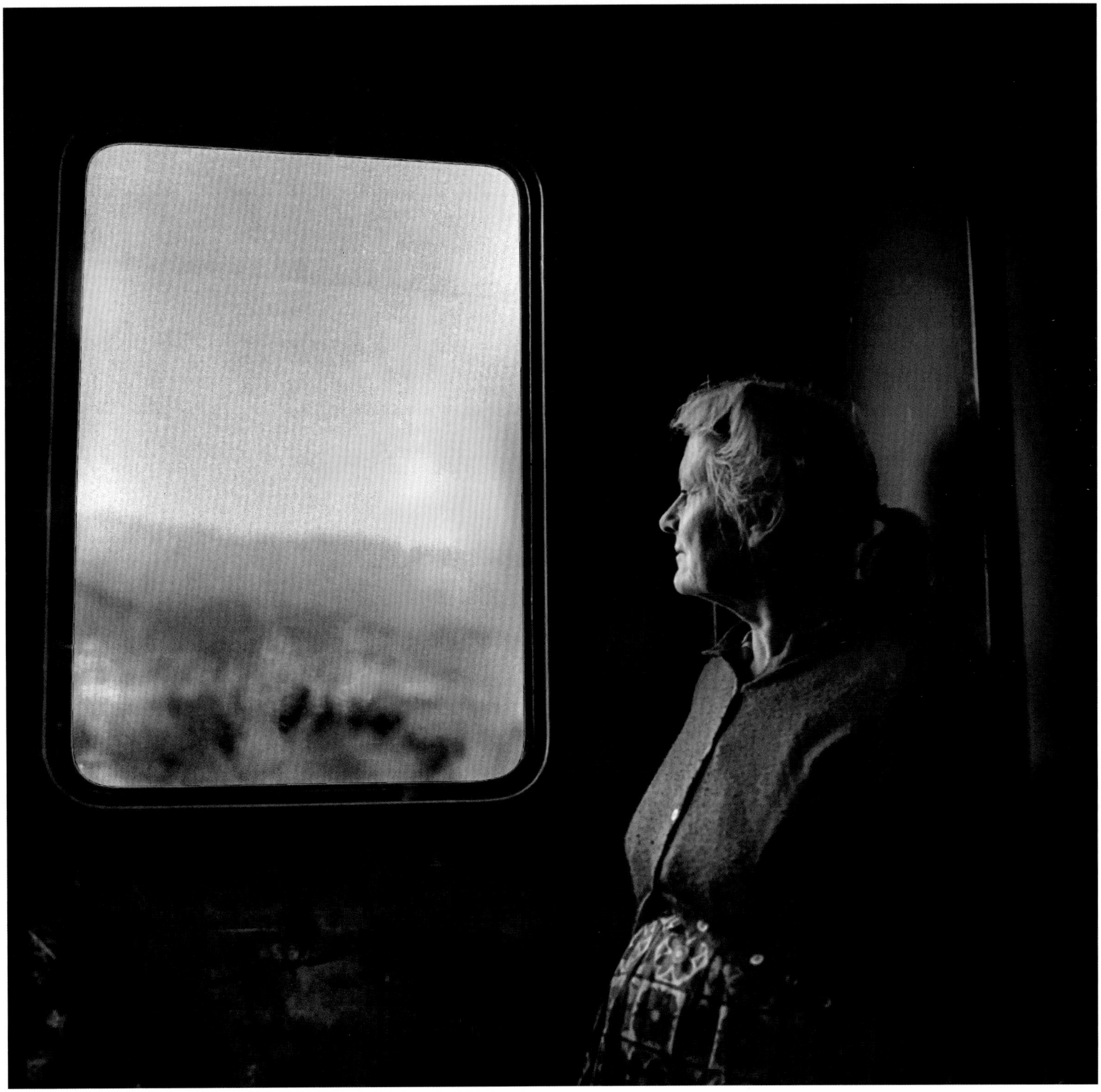

Woman in Train Gangway

ACKNOWLEDGMENTS

The photographs in this book were all but forgotten when I stopped photographing in the mid-1970s. There were many reasons for me putting away my photographic negatives and archives. During the Covid-19 sheltering-in-place mandates in 2020, with the help of my husband, Joe Ramos, I began to digitize my thousands of negatives and also, once again, continued to photograph.

While I was not a fan of social media, I decided to show my photographs on Facebook rather than attempt to create a website. I was very particular about who to befriend on the social media platform and requested friendships with people affiliated with the photography and art world.

Dr. Sally Stein, a noted professor emerita who taught in the Department of Art History at University of California, Irvine, messaged me, which began the journey that led to the publication of this book. I sent her a couple hundred digital files of my photographs from which she put together a strong selection of images that are the basis for this book. Her splendid eye for sequencing and pairing of images into a compelling narrative astonished me. She facilitated presenting the narrative of images to Chronicle Books, which decided to take on the book project. Thank you, Sally, for your support and faith in my work, and thank you for your superlative and insightful essay.

Steven A. Heller, a photographer and writer for *Black & White* photography magazine, messaged me on social media. He told me that he and the magazine's editor, Dean Brierly, were interested in publishing an article about my work. I was both flattered and in disbelief, yet after a series of long email interviews with Stephen, a splendid twelve-page article was published in the October 2022 issue. Thank you, Stephen and Dean, for making the article come to life.

Alida Bray, curator and museum consultant, contacted me after seeing my photographs on social media and offered to curate an exhibition of my photographs at the Sanchez Art Gallery in Pacifica, California. When I brought about a hundred work prints to her at the gallery, she diligently sorted through them and, to my surprise, made a cohesive narrative of about forty of my photographs. Alida, I thank you for curating an excellent exhibition and for your continued support of my photography.

While I don't have an extensive exhibition history, I must thank Margery Mann, photographer, photography historian, and critic. She was a professor at the San Francisco Art Institute and chose a group of my photographs to be part of the *Young Photographers* exhibition, which she curated for the San Francisco Museum of Art (now SFMOMA) in 1971. Several of those images appear in this book. Even though Margery passed away in 1978, I still treasure the memory of her looking at my photographs and how they resonated with her.

Bridget Watson Payne, this book's editor, was a pleasure to work with. It was astonishing to see how Bridget efficiently coordinated so many elements of putting it together. She did so with great patience, understanding, and enthusiasm. She was always there to explain, soothe, support—and did so flawlessly. Thank you, Bridget. And special thanks to Kristen Hewitt and Stella Kim, the exceptional designers, and to the entire support team at Chronicle Books.

Author Rachel Kushner, who spent her teenage years in San Francisco, wrote the introduction for this book, delving into the meaning of some of my photographs. Her comments to do with young people echoed her own adolescent experiences. Thank you, Rachel, for your insights that, in part, helped me to understand those images in a deeper way.

Over the past several difficult years I made many new friends and maintained connections to old friends and family. Thank you all for being there and for understanding and getting what my photographs are about. A special thanks to friend and photography colleague, David Brown.
I would like to thank my husband of forty-nine years, photographer Joe Ramos, for helping me digitize my archives and for his unrelenting devotion to me and this project. We raised two children who have gifted us with wonderful grandchildren and in-laws. Complex familial bonds notwithstanding, we still are lovingly connected.

A special thanks to my muses—the subjects of my photographs who simply lived their lives as I clicked my camera shutter and documented their grand and simple choreographic stances.

—Barbara Ramos, San Francisco, 2024

ABOUT THE CONTRIBUTORS

Barbara Ramos was born in New York City and moved to Los Angeles with her family at the age of six. She received a bachelor of fine arts degree in photography at the San Francisco Art Institute and a master's degree in interdisciplinary creative arts from San Francisco State University. After photographing avidly throughout the early 1970s, Ramos packed away her negatives and took a nearly fifty-year hiatus from the medium to start a handcrafted jewelry business and raise a family. Her work was rediscovered and digitized during the Covid-19 pandemic and gained new acclaim in the world of fine arts and online. She lives in San Francisco with her husband, Joe Ramos, who is also known for his 1970s and 1980s photography.

Rachel Kushner is the bestselling author of *The Mayor of Leipzig*, *The Mars Room*, *The Flamethrowers*, *Telex from Cuba*, *The Strange Case of Rachel K*, and *The Hard Crowd*. She has won the Prix Médicis and been a finalist for the Booker Prize, the National Book Critics Circle Award, the Folio Prize (now known as the Writers' Prize), the James Tait Black Prize, the Dayton Literary Peace Prize, and was twice a finalist for the National Book Award in fiction. She is a Guggenheim Foundation Fellow and the recipient of the Harold D. Vursell Memorial Award from the American Academy of Arts and Letters.

Sally Stein, professor emerita, Department of Art History, University of California, Irvine, is an independent scholar based in Los Angeles. Stein researches and writes about twentieth-century photography in the United States and its relationship to broader questions of culture and society. Her works have covered New Deal president Franklin Delano Roosevelt and Farm Security Administration photographers—in particular Dorothea Lange, Marion Post Wolcott, and Jack Delano. She has also penned numerous essays about popular mass media and the rise of color photography. Stein's research and writing of this essay was supported by a UCI Edward A. Dickson Emeriti Professorship Award.

Steven A. Heller is photographer, educator, and writer. In his photographic practice he is fascinated by alternative format cameras. He has shared his passion as an educator, first for over twenty-five years at the ArtCenter College of Design in Pasadena, California, and then at the Art Institute of California–Hollywood. A contributing writer to *Black & White*, the quarterly fine art photography magazine, Heller has profiled numerous photographers and creative professionals and wrote the first published piece on the life and work of Barbara Ramos.

Library of Congress Cataloging-in-Publication Data

Names: Ramos, Barbara (Photographer), photographer. | Kushner, Rachel, writer of introduction. | Stein, Sally, writer of introduction. | Heller, Steven A., writer of afterword.

Title: A fearless eye : the photography of Barbara Ramos : San Francisco and California, 1969-1973 / essays by Rachel Kushner, Sally Stein, and Steven A. Heller.

Description: San Francisco : Chronicle Books, [2025] | Includes bibliographical references.

Identifiers: LCCN 2024030492 | ISBN 9781797230023 (hardcover)

Subjects: LCSH: Street photography—California—San Francisco. | Portrait photography—California—San Francisco. | San Francisco (California)—History—20th century—Sources.

Classification: LCC TR659.8 .R36 2025 | DDC 779/.40979461—dc23/eng/20240801

LC record available at https://lccn.loc.gov/2024030492

Manufactured in China.

FSC www.fsc.org MIX Paper | Supporting responsible forestry FSC™ C008047

Design by Stella Kim.

Additional image captions:
Page 4: *Two Teenaged Couples at Night*
Page 8: *Daughter and Father at the Academy of Sciences*
Page 15: *Tilt-a-Whirl*

10 9 8 7 6 5 4 3 2 1

Chronicle Books LLC
680 Second Street
San Francisco, California 94107
www.chroniclebooks.com